GROW
MIND
GROW YOUR
LIFE

GROW YOUR MIND GROW YOUR LIFE

7 SIMPLE STRATEGIES
to Increase Focus, Heal Your Pain, and Unlock Your Best Life

DR. NARJES GORJIZADEH

MARBLE BOOK
PUBLISHERS

Published by Marble Book Publishers:
www.marblebookpublishers.com

Cover art: Booksmith Design
Author photography: Simona Janek

 A catalogue record for this work is available from the National Library of Australia

NATIONAL LIBRARY OF AUSTRALIA

Paperback ISBN: 978-0-6451161-0-6

eBook ISBN: 978-0-6451161-1-3

CONTENTS

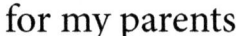

for my parents

Keep walking, though there's
no place to get to. Don't try
to see through the distances.
That's not for human beings.
Move within, but don't move
the way fear makes you move.

—Rumi

FOREWORD

I HAVE KNOWN Dr. Narjes for many years now, and I have seen her go from a woman who was full of stress, anxiety, and health challenges to a woman who is happy, inspirational, and living on purpose every day.

Her transformation has been remarkable!

And in this beautiful book, you will find out how that happened.

Dr. Narjes combines modern science and ancient wisdom and uses her colorful life experiences to guide the reader to a life of health and happiness.

She has written an entertaining and accessible guide on how to heal your body and grow your life so that you can experience a life of good health and more happiness, and graciousness.

Dr. Narjes brings together her decades of training in science as a PhD scientist and beautifully merges it with the deep wisdom she has learned from enlightened teachers, and she presents it to us in a wonderful book of entertaining life lessons and practical techniques.

It carries a simple but powerful message—*when you grow your mind, you will grow your life.* She guides us to let go of negative beliefs and embrace the positive, to believe in our potential and our body's ability to heal, and to live a life of joy and happiness every day.

With easy, practical, and effective tools, this book is a joyful read packed with a ton of thought-provoking content.

I believe this book will inspire and empower every reader to control their own destiny. I recommend this book to anyone looking to create and enjoy a life of health and happiness.

—Vikas Malkani, The Wisdom Coach

INTRODUCTION

IMAGINE YOU WERE granted a superpower that enabled you to choose how you experience life.

What would you choose? Would you choose to experience life as happy or sad? Joyful or frustrating? Peaceful or distressing?

What if I told you that you were born with this superpower?

Yes, you have the ability to *choose*.

There are many things in life that are out of our control. External circumstances may bring us surprises, uncertainties, and unwanted experiences. However, the superpower inside each of us allows us to experience life as happy and joyful regardless of the external circumstances.

The key to unlocking a happy, joyful life, or the life we want, is *inside* us. If we use our superpower, if we assert our ability to choose, we and not the outside world are in control.

But the problem is that most people don't use their superpower.

My aim with this book is to show you how to access and strengthen your superpower with simple strategies so that you can create the life you want.

Choice gives us power. It is our human privilege. And it is available to us in every moment of our lives, even during times when we think we have no options. To unlock the life we want, all we need to do is claim our ability to choose.

When we do, our life will be in our own hands and not in the hands of external situations. Once we use our superpower, there is no obstacle we cannot overcome or limitation we cannot surpass. We can reach our highest potential. And our potential is higher than we think.

There is no limit to how far or high we can soar—unless our mind imposes one. When we grow our mind, we grow our life.

The fact that you picked up this book shows that you want to expand and grow, to use your superpower. I congratulate you for taking a conscious step toward reaching your highest potential.

Once you decide to use your superpower to create what you want and deserve, then even problems, challenges, and uncertainties become opportunities to grow your mind and grow your life.

It may not be immediately apparent to you how a difficult or trying situation could contribute to your growth. But, if you make the choice to see it as an opportunity for life to guide you, you will soon discover how it was a stepping stone to speed up your growth, contributing to your higher, wiser self, not a stone blocking your way.

My life has not been short of challenges. But these challenges were not setbacks. They were the catalysts that advanced my progress toward the wisdom I wanted in my life.

My Path to Growth

Ever since I was a child, I have been searching. I have always wanted to know how life and everything in it happens.

As a young woman, I discovered physics, the study of the how and why of the physical world. I studied physics at university and eventually earned a PhD in materials science with a focus on condensed matter physics. And I pursued a career as a research scientist.

Since the time I began studying for my master's degree, I enjoyed developing computer codes to make the invisible world of atoms visible to the human eye. My simulations showed how atoms move and behave to form increasingly complex structures and how their behavior shapes the behavior of the world we see. They opened a door to an unknown and unseen world. Even though I was creating only a virtual door to a virtual world, the work was exciting and temporarily satisfied my thirst to know.

Over the next several years, my search to understand more about the nature of existence took me on a journey beyond my country and my comfort zone. And it provided me with many opportunities to expand my knowledge of science and of the nature of life itself.

Along the way, there were three unwanted events that at first seemed to nudge me off track but ultimately were the ones that moved me closer toward understanding the world and my role in it.

The first major event was the Tōhoku earthquake in Japan that caused a tsunami and nuclear disaster in 2011. At that time I was working as a research scientist at Tōhoku University, where I had gotten my PhD, and living in the city of Sendai.

The unexpected shake of the earth shook me on the inside as well. Thinking of all the lives lost—people who were living in proximity to me—was difficult for me to digest. Nearly twenty thousand people died as a result of the tsunami that followed the earthquake. I couldn't shake the thought that it could have been me who suddenly disappeared from the earth in the middle of an average day. And it made me question, "Am I really living the life that I want? Would I leave this life feeling fulfilled that I have achieved what I wanted?" And the answer was no.

I had pursued the science and career that I loved, and I could think of no other work that I would have liked to do more. But I was not satisfied. I enjoyed my work. But I knew there was something missing. There was more to the world than current knowledge of physics could explain. And I knew I hadn't found my life's purpose. I knew I had a higher potential inside me to fulfill.

The ground shaking literally beneath my feet showed me how fragile life is and gave me a sense of urgency to find what I'm looking for. I had no clue how to find it, especially since I didn't even know exactly what "it" was, but I knew I had to find it in order to feel fulfilled.

Life helped me. This wake-up call was soon followed by another.

The next major event occurred soon after the earthquake. I went to Singapore to start a new career at a prestigious research institute. I faced a lot of stress at my new workplace. The pressure of adapting to a completely different work environment and work style and the unreasonable expectations of my boss took a mental, emotional, and physical toll on me.

I became more anxious. I couldn't focus. I wasn't productive. I couldn't sleep well. I was unhappy. I had low energy and I was fatigued all the time.

After one year of visiting medical doctors to try to fix these symptoms and feeling no better, I went on a new search to find a solution for managing my stress.

I found it in a meditation class, but that class did so much more than help me relax. It provided a way for me to finally understand the world in a complete and holistic way and, ultimately, revealed my life's purpose.

Since childhood, I had wanted to know how and why things happen. And in my professional life, I searched for this understanding by studying the physical world—the world outside us. Meditation provides this understanding by studying the inner world—the world inside us—by looking at our mind.

Now, with physics and meditation, I had the instruments to see the full view of the world, from the outside and the inside.

I immersed myself in the field of meditation and the science of the mind. By practicing the wisdom and the techniques that I learned, my physical and mental symptoms of stress improved naturally and significantly. These amazing benefits inspired me to want to share what I had learned with others so that they could benefit, too. I became a certified meditation and mindfulness teacher.

Meditation led me to a new path, one exploring my inner world to complement the path I walked exploring the external world in my professional life. I will be forever grateful to my meditation teacher, Vikas Malkani, for introducing me to this path, teaching me the importance of training our mind and focusing on positive thoughts, and helping me to find my life's purpose.

The Curse That Was a Blessing in Disguise

Shortly after I began walking this new path in my journey of life, I moved to Australia.

While working as a research scientist at the University of New South Wales in Sydney, I continued to learn more about the ancient wisdom of meditation and the science of the mind by studying the teachings of ancient and contemporary masters from different parts of the world and exploring the emerging modern scientific research on meditation while practicing a variety of meditation techniques and exploring how my mind affects my life experiences.

I started to see a link between the laws of the physical world and the laws of life. For over a decade now, I had been using computer codes to simulate the building blocks of the physical world. Quantum mechanics was the alphabet of most of my calculations, and calculating the energies of atoms in physical structures was the basis of my simulations. *Energy.* Because when you see the world through the eyes of quantum mechanics, everything is energy. The laws of the physical world and the laws of life are both plays of energy.

This realization helped me understand that there was no gap between my expertise in modern science and ancient wisdom. I was not walking two different paths but the same one.

I started teaching meditation and giving lectures and writing about it in magazines. I had the privilege of finding and following my passion and exploring life from both the inside and the outside. And now it was time to share it with the world. This was my life's purpose: teaching science-based wisdom.

And then, just when I felt complete, I faced the third major event that changed my life. I was diagnosed with a debilitating condition: Lyme disease. Like the earthquake, this diagnosis was a wake-up call reminding me how precious life is.

Lyme disease is caused by an infection from bacteria belonging to the genus *Borrelia*, and it is believed to be transmitted to humans through the bite of an infected tick. I have no memory of ever being bitten by a tick, and my symptoms, such as fatigue, low energy, and difficulty finding words, came on very gradually. I don't know how or when I acquired these bacteria and for how long I had them. It was a long, frustrating journey to get diagnosed, but that was only the beginning of what would become the greatest test of my body and mind.

The wisdom I had gained in the years prior came to my rescue, not only keeping me calm and peaceful and helping my body heal faster but also empowering me to turn this challenge into an opportunity to grow.

In the early, dark days after my diagnosis, I remembered that I had a choice. And I chose to turn this situation into a positive event by seeing and responding to it in that way. Yes, I chose to use my superpower—my ability to choose how I experience life.

I made a decision to use this experience as my unshakable motivation to make the best use of the rest of my life—to grow myself to my highest potential and to help others grow to their highest potential as well. I wanted to have a positive impact in the world.

Soon it was clear that I should write a book—this book—to share my message far and wide, to touch as many lives as possible.

I saw a stronger, wiser, and happier Narjes waiting for me on the other side of this challenge. This future self became my guardian over the following months as I went through the ups and downs of several different treatments and all the mental, emotional, and physical pain they caused. No matter what happened or how I felt, I kept my focus on this future Narjes.

The treatments used to try to clear my body of the bacteria exacerbated my physical symptoms, such as fatigue, and caused new, uncomfortable emotions. Fear, anxiety, worry, agitation, and sadness would suddenly hit me out of nowhere.

I had never known fear like this before. I often felt, even safe in my home, as if a tiger was chasing me and I was running for my life. I would wake up in the morning with my heart pounding in my chest, by body overwhelmed with anxiety. I didn't know exactly what I was anxious about, what I was afraid of. I was just anxious. I was just afraid.

Using my superpower helped me navigate these challenges. The vision of my healed future self never left me. She patiently accompanied me every step of the way, assuring me that she was there for me until we could be one and the same. When I was struggling, this future Narjes would reach her hand out and pull me into the air to breathe. When I was planning talks and writing articles about meditation or taking notes for my book, this future Narjes would clap her hands, cheering me up and encouraging me to continue. When I was in pain or discomfort because of the treatments for Lyme disease, this future Narjes would give me an assuring and peaceful smile to let me know that it would all pass away soon and I would be united with her.

The key to becoming that future self was to keep my focus on it.

I realized that I could manage any discomfort when I remain focused—focused on the present moment, focused on the ancient wisdom of meditation, and focused on my healed self.

So, I used all I had learned during my years exploring the science of the mind and everything I knew about physics and modern science to find strategies to keep my focus on the things that would empower me stay calm and peaceful in the present moment, prepare me to live my desired future, and help my body heal itself faster.

I started experimenting with different strategies to test their effectiveness in reducing mental, emotional, and physical pain. I found many powerful ones.

In this book, I share these simple strategies, the wisdom behind them, and the science of how and why such basic techniques are effective at healing pain and unlocking the life we want.

Because they are so simple, the effectiveness of these strategies was unbelievably surprising to me. There were days when my mind would get overwhelmed with fear, worry, anxiety, or agitation, but by using one of the seven strategies discussed in part 2, I was able to calm my mind, turn it toward the positive again, and reduce the negative emotions significantly, sometimes within just a few minutes. There were times when I was racked by physical pain, but I could reduce it, sometimes significantly, by using one of my strategies and keeping my focus on positive and empowering thoughts.

Being present in the moment and focusing your mind on the positives are the most loving ways to heal your pain, whether it's mental, emotional, or physical pain. You can change your experience of life, even pain, if you choose to.

Two years after the diagnosis of Lyme disease, I was symptom-free. I underwent medical treatment for nine months and spent the rest of that time using acupuncture to help my body restore its balance and heal itself. The simple strategies to keep my mind focused on the present moment and on my ideal future played a key role in my rapid recovery.

During this time, I continued teaching, writing, and giving talks, and I became a life coach to empower more people to create the life they want. I also created my coaching program, called the G.R.O.W. program—Get clarity, Respond, Optimize, Wisdom— to help others grow their happiness, grow their productivity, and remove their stress.

I've been sharing my wisdom and tools for three years now and I have touched thousands of people around the world with my programs, talks, presentations, coaching, and articles. With this book, I hope to help you, too.

How This Book Will Help You

The strategies in this book helped me heal my pain and unlock my best future despite many challenges. They have helped many others heal their pain as well. I believe they will do the same for you, whether you are struggling with stress, anxiety, negative thinking, unhappiness, lack of focus, fear of uncertainty, physical pain or health issues, or you seek to move toward greater health, greater happiness, and greater life satisfaction.

The simple strategies I will share can be used in your everyday life as well as in difficult situations or during stressful events (such as job loss, divorce, chronic disease, or a financial setback) to keep you focused, calm, positive, and more productive.

These strategies are not only helpful but also necessary in today's fast-paced life to keep us sane and peaceful.

We are living in an interesting time. We have more material comfort than previous generations, but we don't seem to be happier or more fulfilled. We have pain. We live with mental and emotional pain that may lead to health issues and physical pain if they remain ignored and unresolved.

Speed is the pain that we all share.

In today's modern lifestyle, the pace of life is getting faster and faster. Our mind is occupied with the endless stream of information it receives from our digital, online world. The speed of modern life is taking a toll on us, making us less focused. It causes us to pass through the moments of each day without paying attention to them. By missing the moments of our life, we are missing life itself.

We are getting so used to having an overstimulated mind and living life as if we were running a race that we are forgetting the art of slowing down, relaxing, and enjoying life for the sake of living. We hardly have time for ourselves, for things that truly matter in life, and for *living* our lives.

The pain of being disconnected from ourselves, others, and life results in mental, emotional, and physical tension in almost every single one of us. Maybe you.

Slowing down to connect with the individual moments in your life reduces speed and increases focus, joy, and happiness. The strategies shared in this book are simple ways to help the mind slow down and learn to focus.

With a focused mind, you can heal your pain and pave the way toward your best life. You will enjoy your life and create the one you want with less struggle, less stress, and more efficiency. You will be inspired to follow your dreams and eradicate the limiting beliefs that block you from your best future.

The seven strategies are simple, effective, and quick, and they easily fit into any busy schedule. Most of them take no longer than the length of one breath. The key is to do them repeatedly.

Every moment is an opportunity to develop the ability to focus. There are strategies that you can choose to do right in the morning when you wake up to set the tone of your mind for a happy, positive, and productive day. And there are different strategies to use throughout the day to keep you anchored in the moment and enhance the quality of your day, whether you are at home, at work, in your car, waiting on a line, in between meetings, taking a walk, or drinking a coffee.

Many of these strategies are ones that I created or modified by blending my understanding of quantum physics, neuroscience, wisdom, and techniques of meditation. They are science-based techniques inspired by ancient wisdom and adapted for our modern world.

If you are an overscheduled professional running from one meeting (or Zoom call) to another, a busy parent juggling work and home responsibilities, a manager who needs to make important decisions for your company in the middle of a chaotic day, or a person with chronic pain, these strategies will help you be and perform at your best.

What This Book Is and Is Not

This book is not about meditation. It will introduce you to a new way of thinking and provide simple, quick, and effective techniques for enhancing your focus and training your mind to stay positive.

They are like micro push-ups to keep your mind and brain fit.

If you have a meditation practice, you can use these techniques to support it by helping to keep you anchored in the moment.

How To Use This Book

Part 1 is your foundation, explaining what we need to live a happy and thriving life in our modern world and how each of the seven strategies address those needs. You'll also learn the science behind the strategies.

The chapters in part 2 will introduce you to each of the strategies and provide you with everything you need to know to start using them right away. With step-by-step instructions and examples of the strategies in action, you'll feel confident using each one to focus your mind, appreciate the present moment, and unlock the future you want.

Because the strategies build on one another I suggest reading the chapters in chronological order. Once you're familiar with all seven, you can pick and choose which one (or a combination of them) to practice as part of your daily routine or use during a challenging time. One strategy may work better than another in a certain situation or when you are in a specific mood. With these seven strategies in your toolbox, you will always find one that works no matter what you are confronting.

By the end of the book, you'll be ready to bloom into your future self.

Embarking on Your Journey

Are you ready to unlock your best life one moment at a time?

I may not know the specific pain you are struggling with right now, but whether it is the stress of navigating through daily activities or of an immediate crisis, I want you to know that I understand your pain. And I assure you that there is a way out of it. The way through is you. Your inner superpower, your ability to choose to focus your mind on how you wish to experience life, is available to you now and always.

I'm with you on every step of this journey, from easing your present pain to shaping your future.

Your best future is closer than you think, the universe is more supportive than you imagine, and your focus is more powerful than you know.

As you embark, visualize your healed, pain-free self and your best future.

Now, turn the page and let's begin.

Part One

Life Is Growth

CHAPTER 1

THREE PILLARS TO GROWTH

I WAS SITTING on a bench in the pavilion on the hill. The gentle touch of the cool morning breeze was taking away the sleep from my eyes. I could hear the leaves of the trees near me dancing with the breeze. Breathing the fresh air was bringing me back to my senses and reminding my mind to allow space for some rest. I could see the city of Sendai waking up to start a new day below me.

I had woken up early this morning and couldn't go back to sleep. So, I jumped onto my bike and rode to the crest of the hill near my apartment. It was my secret place where I came to bathe in its mysteriously peaceful air whenever I felt overwhelmed by the busyness of the world and my mind.

It was a small hill, but it was high enough that I could see a large part of Sendai from above.

I'd park my bike at the foot of the hill then walk up the long staircase to the top. A modest courtyard greeted me, with a few statues and trees scattered here and there. There was a small shrine in the middle of the courtyard. Sometimes a person or two would come to worship.

But I'd go there to watch the city from above and relax, slipping into this place's calming atmosphere.

On this morning, I'd walked up an additional few stairs from the right corner of the courtyard to reach a small pavilion with a panoramic view of the city. Sitting on one of the two benches in the pavilion, I saw the city stretching to the forest-covered hills. I could see the river I crossed to get here and the wide sidewalks and trees along the river. Cars and buses filled the streets. A few people were walking.

The activities of the day were getting started. But I was here, high above all those activities, simply watching.

My worries about my PhD project ebbed into a sense of serenity and well-being that I'd finish the project on time. After about an hour sitting there, I was calm and ready to go down the hill and start my day, refreshed and recharged.

This experience is a metaphor for what this book is about: to take ourselves out of the routine and activities of our daily lives for a moment, to refresh our mind and our view of life.

By doing so, we are reenergized and able to be and do our best. By taking ourselves out of the activity in our mind for a moment and pausing the negative thoughts that lead to negative emotions, we reconnect with the peace inside us that supports our highest potential.

In Search of Growth

Watching the activity occurring in the city below me and not participating in it gave me the space to contemplate life on a deeper level. Though I didn't realize it yet, I was connecting with an invisible dimension of life on that hilltop. Connection was something I'd desired ever since I was a child.

Ever since I can remember, I have wanted to know about the how and why of life and the universe.

In childhood, I'd pay attention to the details of how things happen in nature around me. I'd spend an hour watching the waves in the sea, wondering how they were created, imagining the merging forces of water and wind making this part of the sea rise and then collapse.

I wanted to know what moves things—Earth, the sun, the clouds, the leaves on the trees. I asked endless questions. What is time? What is eternity? Where does the universe end? How does this whole thing work?

I was born and grew up in Iran in a family that valued learning and provided me with the best resources and opportunities available to learn and grow. Books were my best friends and my treasure. One of my most prized was a collection of Persian poems. It was filled with a wealth of wisdom from great masters such as Rumi, Hafiz, and Saadi. I especially liked the works of Rumi, the great Sufi poet.

I'd read the poems of Rumi and the other great poets trying to understand their message. Even though I knew I couldn't understand the depth of their meaning, these poems, through their words and images, sought to explain the mystery of life. So, I spent a significant amount of time contemplating the mystery in the words of the masters and the veil of mystery covering almost everything around me.

Years passed and the mystery remained a mystery. However, I continued the practice of contemplation in the hope that I might still unravel it. My thirst to know remained. My quest continued. I kept seeking.

Looking back, I see my quest and a map buried inside of me. I couldn't see the map then, but it was there, guiding me and the decisions that shaped my life.

A crucial step in growing to our highest potential is leaving behind the old and familiar and going to the new and unfamiliar. If the branch of a tree wants to grow, it must stretch into a space it hasn't been before, it must go into the unknown.

The map led me to Japan. Since I was a girl, I'd always wanted to visit Japan. I liked learning about it and its culture. So, after completing my master's degree at Sharif University of Technology, the top university in Iran, I applied for and received a scholarship for a PhD in computational materials science with a focus on condensed matter physics from the Institute for Materials Research at Tōhoku University, Japan. It was ranked first in the world in this field at that time.

Moving to a new country was an amazing opportunity for me to grow. A crucial step in growing to our highest potential is leaving behind the old and familiar and going to the new and unfamiliar.

If the branch of a tree wants to grow, it must stretch into a space it hasn't been before, it must go into the unknown.

It might be scary, difficult, or challenging. But the growth that results from stretching brings contentment and fulfillment. We might feel secure where we are, but there is something within us that is longing to expand, longing to grow, longing to reach into the unknown. It won't let us settle down. It won't let us be content unless we fulfill its wishes to explore beyond the known.

My longing to expand took me to Japan. My experience of the unknown in Japan was full of excitement. Every encounter was an opportunity to experience something new. From the bite of each meal to the way to greet and speak and commute, everything was an adventure. And I loved it. I began to love Japan and the Japanese culture. I started to grow more and more in this new world.

One of the places that attracted me was that hilltop near my apartment. My natural inclination to spend time there was, in some way, preparing me for my biggest breakthrough yet to come.

At that time, I thought it was important to have an active mind, thinking and contemplating nonstop. When I'd get overwhelmed by the constant activity of my mind, I was drawn to my secret place on the hilltop to silence my mind and connect with a mysterious sense of peace that would visit me there.

I did not notice that Japan is the country of Zen, a way of meditation. On the surface Zen may not seem related to my childhood interest in Persian poetry, but both originate from enlightened masters who understood life in its entirety. The methods of expressing what they know may be different, but they both point out the same thing: the truth about life. And that was what I had always wanted to know—the how and why of life and everything in it.

However, I didn't learn about Zen or meditation in the nearly seven years that I lived in Japan. I didn't know that the understanding I was seeking required more than just the science of the physical world. Learning about the physical laws of the universe and the phenomena of the physical world was so magnificent that I never thought what I was looking for lay beyond the physical sciences.

My mind was not ready to learn about Zen and meditation while I was studying for my PhD. But in that courtyard perched high above Sendai, I was noticing that by watching daily activity from above and seeing but not participating in it for a while I was able to let my mind soak in a sense of serenity.

These moments revealed the power of pause, a valuable lesson to me and one of the pillars that supports the strategies in this book.

There are three pillars that underlie the strategies in this book: *pause*, *wisdom*, and *focus*.

The First Pillar: Pause

Taking a small pause between the activities of our day-to-day life refreshes our mind and recharges us, enhancing our ability to live our lives to the fullest. When we know how to take a moment to pause, to distance ourselves from the rush of our mind, we connect with the sense of peace inside us that refreshes our body, heart, mind, and soul. These moments make us more relaxed, productive, and able to unlock the life we want.

As strange as it may sound, rest is the basis of activity. Without sufficient rest, we're not as productive as we could be. We know this by experience. When we don't have a good night's sleep, we do not have sufficient energy for the day ahead.

In these moments of pause, you can become conscious of your thoughts and beliefs, your dreams about your future, and how you see your present moment if you choose to. Are they positive or negative? Are they supporting your way toward your best life or blocking your way? By shifting the focus of your mind from what's blocking your way to what supports you, you gain access to your highest potential and the life you want.

> Taking a small pause between the activities of our day-to-day life refreshes our mind and recharges us, enhancing our ability to live our lives to the fullest.

Each moment of pause adds up, drop by drop, to create a tide moving you toward your best life: relaxed, productive, and as you desire. You don't need to take big steps to see big results. You do need *persistence* to repeat small steps over and over to create the life you want and enjoy the life you deserve.

In nature, a single drop of water can change the form of a rock. If a drop of water falls on the surface of a rock over and over and over, it can make a dent on the surface. The secret is simply in its persistence. There is no effort or tension or drive from the drop to try to change the rock. Simply by repeating a single act of falling on the rock on the same spot, over a period of time, a dent starts to appear.

In the same way, moments of pause can change our lives. We'll harness the power of pause in each of the strategies in this book.

The Second Pillar: Wisdom

Being strong like a rock does not equal power any more than being flexible like water indicates weakness. The wise know when to be strong and when to be flexible. In other words, wisdom is knowing how to have the right combination of strength and flexibility.

When we hold on to our emotions tension accumulates inside us. If we don't release it, one day we reach a point where our minds and our bodies break down.

One of the most inspiring examples of this wisdom is the way the Japanese earthquake-proof buildings are constructed. I was familiar with this concept intellectually, but I realized its power when I experienced the powerful earthquake that hit Japan on March 11, 2011.

It was 2:46 in the afternoon when the first tremors started. I was standing in front of the building at Tōhoku University, where I was working. I had gone to lunch with my husband, Farshid, later than usual that day. I was about to say bye and go back to work when the ground beneath our feet started to shake.

Earthquakes are a regular event in Japan and we were used to them. But this one was far from usual. It was so strong that I could hardly keep my balance while standing. And it was exceptionally long. The earth shook angrily, as if it were emptying all of the suppressed emotions it had accumulated over a long, hard time.

Before moving on to the lesson of flexibility and strength, I want to point out a crucial lesson we can take from earthquakes that is related to the importance of taking a pause—the first pillar.

An earthquake is a release of tension, disbursing the energy that has been accumulated between rocks that are pushing against each other. They are trying to move but are stuck together. Tension builds up and reaches a point at which the rocks can't hold it any longer, and so they break apart. The energy is transferred to the surface of the earth and is released. Tension is released and the rocks continue moving until they get stuck again.

> Introducing frequent moments of pause throughout your day to give your mind a rest between your daily activities helps to relieve tension and bring your mind and body closer to their ideal relaxed state.

This is how tension affects our minds and our bodies as well.

When we hold on to our emotions tension accumulates inside us. If we don't release it, one day we reach a point where our minds and our bodies break down. Release of tension inside the earth or inside us is nature's way to help the system get closer to a more relaxed state. However, we can prevent the tension inside us from accumulating.

Introducing frequent moments of pause throughout your day to give your mind a rest between your daily activities helps to relieve tension and bring your mind and body closer to their ideal relaxed state. Like a drop of water that can change the rock, the effect of each moment of pause adds up to make a change in the quality of our life.

Now, this earthquake I was experiencing that day was a release of a powerful force that had accumulated over a long period of time. Over the course of my nearly seven years in Japan, I frequently heard that there is a major earthquake in Sendai every thirty years, and it was overdue. Some of my Japanese friends were worried that the more time that passed meant the inevitable earthquake would be of a high magnitude.

They were right to be worried. The 2011 earthquake was the most powerful earthquake ever recorded in Japan. It was so strong that it shifted the axis of Earth, increased Earth's rotational speed, and moved the entire mainland of Japan.

While I struggled to stay on my feet during such a powerful earthquake, I was amazed to witness the surrounding buildings standing strong. I saw tiles fall from the roofs of some buildings. Cracks appeared in several. But none collapsed or sustained serious damage. With modest repair, the buildings were as good as new and ready to withstand the next earthquake.

> Just as we can't prevent earthquakes, we can't avoid difficulties and challenges in life altogether. They happen unexpectedly to all of us. You can't prevent them, but you can earthquake-proof yourself.

Some of those buildings were nearly a hundred years old, and yet there they were, standing strong even after such an exceptionally punishing quake. I was amazed and took the lesson to heart: to remain upright we must be flexible.

Even the strongest material has a breaking point. How to make a building strong enough to withstand earthquakes then? Design them to absorb the energy of the quake, so that the strong materials feel less force and can stand steady. Add flexibility to rigidity. This is the Japanese secret to earthquake-proof buildings.

The approach has its origins in the ancient engineering wisdom that built five-story pagodas to be exceptionally earthquake resistant. These buildings, at major temples in Japan, are made masterfully from wood, with hardly any nails. There is no record of any Japanese pagoda, some as old as thirteen hundred years, ever collapsing in an earthquake.

The secret is in their internal architectural design.

The key to the pagoda's outstanding quake resistance is believed to be a single large pillar at the core of the building that runs from deep within the foundation to beyond the rooftop. This pillar is not attached to the structure of the building. It absorbs the shake from the foundation without transferring the shake to the building. In addition to the core pillar, the joints of the building are designed in such a way that they absorb the shake and dampen the force. These two elements add flexibility to the structure.

This genius design is a metaphor for how we can remain stable on the inside when the outside world is shaking. Life is sometimes unstable. We might encounter adversity, the loss of a loved one, financial strain, natural disasters, breakups, job loss, poor health, an accident, or the stress of daily living. All these factors shake us from the inside. They may cause uncomfortable emotions that are unpleasant to face.

Just as we can't prevent earthquakes, we can't avoid difficulties and challenges in life altogether. They happen unexpectedly to all of us. You can't prevent them, but you can earthquake-proof yourself.

Like a pagoda, you can stand strong even during the biggest shake-ups of life. All you need is a core pillar that knows how to absorb the unwanted quakes.

That core pillar is wisdom, the wisdom to see ourselves and the world around us, and to know how to interact with the world with both strength and flexibility. Wisdom is the shock absorber that earthquake-proofs us so we can go through life with more

> Where your mind lands is where you will eventually land. It is important to focus on what you want instead of what you don't want, what you have instead of what you don't have, and what you can do instead of what you can't do.

calmness, peace, and joy even when our life is shaking.

Wisdom is the core pillar that absorbs the force of the negative events, negative thoughts, and negative emotions that shake us from inside. It keeps us stable so that we can remain peaceful, resilient, and productive. It empowers us to stand strong in life and reach our highest potential and live the life we want, regardless of whether or not life

brings strong earthquakes.

Wisdom is the second pillar of the strategies in this book and the core pillar. Each strategy will help you gain the wisdom to become stronger and more flexible and able to absorb the shakes of life.

The Third Pillar: Focus

Where your mind lands is where you will eventually land. That is why focus is the third pillar of the strategies in this book. With a focused mind, you can focus on what you choose. Otherwise, a mind that does not know how to focus will get distracted and land on unwanted things.

It is important to focus on what you want instead of what you don't want, what you have instead of what you don't have, and what you can do instead of what you can't do.

The ability to focus our minds is especially important when life is shaking us and stirring our emotions.

Soon after the earthquake I faced challenges that seriously shook me and stirred my emotions.

I went to Singapore ten days after the earthquake to start a new career there. Singapore is one of the best countries in the world to live in. It is one of the safest and cleanest with a high quality of life and standard of living. I loved the country, but I was facing a lot of stress at my new job.

I was working at a prestigious research institute in the most high-tech building in the city with great facilities and talented researchers. However, I felt under pressure to adjust to a different working style that I believed was limiting my creativity to do research. Even though my boss was a great person and an amazing scientist, I felt that she was trying a little too much to control my work and how I did it. Her frequent criticism only added to my daily stress load.

Lacking a core pillar of wisdom, I started focusing on all the things that I didn't want in my workplace.

Stress affected my mind and eventually my physical health. Both started deteriorating. Each day, I was becoming unhappier. I was fatigued all the time, and the quality of my sleep was getting worse.

All this sent me on a search to find a solution for my stress. That's when I found meditation and the science of the mind and the way to understand the world and everything in it that I had been looking for since childhood.

Through meditation, I learned many things that changed my life. Two of the most important were how to focus and what to focus on.

I came to understand that I am responsible for my life, and I determine how I experience it—that whatever I'm feeling is created by me because it all starts in my mind. Finding the root cause of things was always my interest. And now I had found something that promised to reveal why we feel the way we do about our lives—and how to change it. Our mind is the root of our life experiences. By upgrading our mind we would upgrade our life.

I came to understand how I was creating my problems in my own mind. I was resisting being controlled by my boss, believing that I should be free. Through the wisdom of meditation, I realized that being free does not mean controlling the outside environment so it is exactly the way you want it. The outside world is not always in your control. But you can always be in charge of your inner world.

Being free means having the freedom of choice, the freedom to choose *how* you respond to the outside world based on what you *want*. This choice is always in your hands. If you want to be happy, you are always free to *choose* happiness, to *be* happy, regardless of what's happening in the outside world.

> Choice is your superpower and your privilege as a human being. By growing your mind and knowing how to use your privilege of choice, you grow your life.

If someone can determine how you feel on the inside through a compliment or an insult, then the outside world is determining how you feel, not you. Real freedom is choosing to be happy even when someone is insulting you, because you know the control button to your interior, your experience of life, is in your power and not anyone else's.

The power to choose resides in your mind.

Choice is your superpower and your privilege as a human being. By growing your mind and knowing how to use your privilege of choice, you grow your life.

Through meditation, I realized that choice was always available to me. Instead of focusing on what I don't want and trying to control what I can't control (outside circumstances), I shifted my mind to focus on what I want and control what I can control (my inside).

Instead of focusing on thoughts such as "I don't want to work like this" and exaggerating the difficult aspects of the situation in my mind, I started choosing to shift my focus to other aspects of my life that empowered me and made me happy.

Once I chose not to participate in creating problems, there were no problems. I could see that the "problem" was simply that my boss and I had a difference of opinion about how work should be done. Besides, I had a certain expectation of how my boss should be and she had a certain expectation of how her employee should be. Our expectations were not met, and that led to our frustration.

As masters of wisdom say, it is wiser to cover your feet with leather than try to cover the entire earth with leather. Before gaining the wisdom of meditation, I had been trying to cover the earth with leather. I was expecting the outside world to be the way I like it so that I can be happy. Now I began the practice of covering my feet. I began to choose what I want to focus on in my mind.

With this wisdom, my mind shifted from focusing on all the things that I didn't want to the good things that I already had and the positive things that I wanted. With wisdom, my mind started to grow, expanding to consciously look for the blessings in my life.

Whenever I focused on my blessings, I felt happy. Whenever I lost my focus, my mind would start wandering to all of the things that I didn't want and my so-called problems. But, as my meditation practice deepened, I became better able to identify when my mind started wandering and how to return its focus to what upgraded my life experience.

Techniques of meditation train the mind to focus. When you train your mind to stay focused, your mind slows down, decreasing the sense of rushing and the wandering. Then, you will have more control over where your mind lands and you can direct it to stay focused on what you choose.

Even if you are facing challenges or uncertainties, hold your focus on the work you enjoy, imagine your best future, and do whatever you can in the moment to make that future closer. Focus brings joy to your present moment and smooths the way to your desired future.

Happiness Is Here Not There

As I progressed in the techniques and understanding the wisdom of meditation, I also realized that I hadn't been happy and content because I was looking for them in all the wrong places.

For years, I had been looking for happiness and contentment in achievements, success, accomplishment, and relationships. Contentment was always one step ahead, waving me on to the next new goal.

I had been chasing happiness on the outside. Everything I thought would bring me happiness—a thriving career and marriage, for example—were good for their own sake, made my life more comfortable, and added to a sense that "I did it," but I should not have mistaken them for happiness.

Happiness is not something out there, existing in the outside world to be chased. Happiness is something inside each one of us, available right now. We can be happy right now, regardless of our life circumstances—if we choose to be.

As my study of the science of the mind deepened, I came to understand that happiness is not something out there, existing in the outside world to be chased. Happiness is something inside each one of us, available right now. We can be happy right now, regardless of our life circumstances—if we choose to be. In this moment, we have everything required to be happy. But we never really live *in this moment*. Our minds are too distracted. We are either one step ahead in the future or one step behind in the past.

With practice of focus I could stay in the present moment. I could close my eyes, sit in peace, and watch the activity of my mind, observing it from above, like my mornings high above Sendai. My mind would calm down and a sense of peace would surround me and I would feel refreshed and recharged. With focus, I was happy, peaceful, and relaxed.

There are no circumstances in life that can stop you from growing into your higher self. Even if a situation seems to be blocking what you wish to do, look further. Maybe what you want to achieve in this life is even bigger than what you had thought.

I could also direct the stories in my mind to play out the future that I wanted instead of playing out the past that I didn't want. I was becoming more conscious. I was becoming the conscious creator of my own life.

The ability to stay focused is a key quality that is required to create the life we truly want and enjoy. That is why focus is the third pillar of the strategies in this book.

The strategies will show you simple techniques to train your mind to remain in the here and now, where happiness is available, and become the conscious creator of your own life.

The Three Pillars Support You and Help You Grow

With the pillars of *pause*, *wisdom*, and *focus* my inner building has remained stable and strong and I have become more in control of my mind, my thoughts, and my emotions.

The core pillar of wisdom along with the pillars of pause and focus came to my rescue and helped me remain strong, purposeful, and stable during the biggest tremor in my life.

When I first heard my Lyme disease diagnosis, I went into a state of shock that paralyzed my mind for two days. I was lost in the darkness of my fear over the uncertainty of my future with this disease. But after those two days, my core pillar of wisdom started working.

I realized that I knew I had a choice. If I chose, I could transform this challenging situation. I relied on my wisdom and I made my decision: "I will make this the best event of my life."

There are no circumstances in life that can stop you from growing into your higher self. Even if a situation seems to be blocking what you wish to do, look further. Maybe what you want to achieve in this life is even bigger than what you had thought. Wisdom helps you see all life situations, even significant obstacles, as opportunities to grow.

And when you introduce a moment of pause and focus your mind on the empowering thoughts that wisdom suggests to you, you can turn all life situations into opportunities for growth.

When I faced my biggest shake in life, I realized the value of each moment. It is important to enjoy every moment, because once they are gone they are gone; they are never coming back. Each moment lost is a missed opportunity to enjoy *life*. What is life without each and every one of these moments? While we are focusing on the things that are going wrong in our life, we are missing out on enjoying the good things that *are* present in the moment.

The three pillars empowered me to not only enjoy my moments in spite of the challenges but to also look beyond myself and help others enjoy their lives, too.

I realized that I won't feel fulfilled unless I include others in my life and make an impact in other people's lives.

Life is a continuous sharing and exchange of energies. The trees breathe in carbon dioxide and breathe out oxygen; and we breathe in oxygen and breathe out carbon dioxide. This cycle is needed for energy to flow. Otherwise energy will stagnate. If you breathe in and don't breathe out, life ends. If you breathe out and don't breathe in, life ends. Life ceases if sharing ceases.

> You can heal your pains and unlock your best life one moment of pause at a time, one word of wisdom at a time, and one drop of focus at a time.

What I received from others, I should give to others for the cycle to be complete. That's the way to a whole and fulfilled life. So, I decided to share what I've learned about pause, wisdom, and focus with as many people as I can to change lives for the better and help more people live their best life. And the joy that I found in sharing this treasure is priceless.

When you face a problem, if you see yourself as part of a bigger identity, you will expand yourself beyond yourself. You grow yourself beyond your boundaries and beyond yourself.

The three pillars—pause, wisdom, and focus—empower you to grow your mind, your life, and the lives of others.

The strategies in this book use these three pillars:

1. **Pause**. These strategies require you to take a pause. Take a moment to pause and let your mind have a moment of rest and recharge. In this pause, use the next two pillars.

2. **Wisdom**. Wisdom is understanding ourselves and the world around us and knowing how to interact with it. It is the core pillar that keeps your inner building stable as you navigate everyday life as well as times of uncertainty and challenge. It encourages us to be strong and flexible, able to constantly grow.

   Each of the strategies will help you gain wisdom that grows your mind. Your mind determines the quality of your life. With wisdom, you'll be equipped to be in charge of your mind and create the life that *you* want regardless of what the outside circumstances in life might bring you.

   I'll share the ancient wisdom and modern science behind each strategy and why it's so effective. With this knowledge, you'll expand your mind and upgrade the way you see life and interact with it.

3. **Focus**. Each strategy requires you to focus. They teach you what to focus on and they strengthen your ability to do so. Namely, to consciously focus on what empowers you and recharges your mind, your body, and your soul.

These pillars are like a breeze that cools down the speed and sense of rush in your mind, and they create a space in your mind to release tension from your mind and your body. They keep your mind focused on the positive aspects of life, and they empower you be at your best and use your highest potential to unlock the life you want and create the best life experiences for yourself.

You can heal your pains and unlock your best life one moment of pause at a time, one word of wisdom at a time, and one drop of focus at a time.

In the next chapter I explain why it is important today more than ever before to have these qualities and to implement these strategies.

CHAPTER 2

FROM SURVIVAL MODE TO CONSCIOUS MODE

ONE EVENING, a year after I moved to Australia, I was working on my computer in my office at the university. My desk was next to a glass wall, so I could see the trees outside the building with a slight turn of my head. In fact, I would often take a pause to look outside at the trees and connect with the beauties of nature to keep myself grounded.

At that particular moment, I was focused on my work but suddenly I noticed that the light coming from the outside was changing color. The whitish light turned into a bright yellowish light. At the same time, a chorus of birds started singing. I looked outside. It was magical.

It had been raining the whole day and the sky was covered with thick clouds. But the rain had stopped and now the last rays of sun were shining on the wet tree leaves. When the glistening leaves moved in the gentle breeze it was as if thousands of diamonds sprinkled the trees.

I guessed there would be a rainbow soon. So, I got up to go outside and see it. As I walked down the hall, I passed many people working in their offices, all with glass doors and floor-to-ceiling windows, along the way. No one else seemed to be aware of the magical moment unfolding outdoors. They were too busy discussing projects, reading, or tapping away at their computer keyboard.

I left the building and I saw the most beautiful sky that I have ever seen. A beautiful rainbow stretched across the sky. Even more magical than the rainbow was the sunset. The sun's yellow rays penetrated the thick clouds from two places next to each other, as if there were two massive fires in the sky. The clouds surrounding these two fires appeared orange in color with some shadows of pink that would fade away in a background of violet clouds. The sky was a piece of art like no other.

But the ground, too, was a work of art. The wet ground of the walkway leading to the main gate of the university was reflecting the sky. This colorful carpet, lined with trees on both sides of the path, the vibrant sky above, and the music of the singing birds created an unforgettable moment.

Some students graduated against the backdrop of this amazing scene, capturing the beauty in photos with their diplomas and parents.

It was a special moment. However, I would have missed this beauty if I hadn't taken a pause during my workday to look outside, recognized the value of such a moment for me, even though everyone else ignored it, and focused on the joy it brought to me. I went back to work with a big smile on my face and in my heart and my soul. Excited and pumped with energy, I finished my work quicker than I expected.

For all the magic in that moment, it was an ordinary moment of an ordinary day for the people who were sitting in their offices looking at their screens with their backs to the window. They were unaware of the beauty available to them in that brief moment.

Before I learned to appreciate the three pillars of pause, wisdom, and focus, I was one of those people who had lost the connection to the magic in life. I spent whole days inside my office, living in the world of my mind, *thinking* about the universe, while I was missing out on *living* in this universe, looking at the sky, listening to the whispers of the leaves dancing by the breeze, imbibing the magic of life and the beauty all around me.

This is how most of us live our lives. Magical things happen in each moment, but we miss them, because we don't pay attention to them. We skip the moment we are in to go to the next one. We are always on fast-forward.

The speed of modern living pushes the fast-forward button even more and distracts us from *being* and from *living*.

The Speed of Modern Living

The pace of modern life is getting faster and faster. The constant sense of rush and over-busyness in our minds is growing more overwhelming. We are becoming wired to distract ourselves from the present moment that we live in and skip to the next one, and the next and the next. We are becoming wired to miss life as we live it. As Osho, the contemporary mystic, said missing becomes our habit. Missing life becomes our habit. The fast pace of life is leaving a mark on our minds, our brains, and our bodies.

While we have more physical comforts than any generation in human history, we are not the happiest or healthiest. Stress, anxiety, and depression are rampant. We are living life without connecting with life, and that hurts.

In the modern world, the digital revolution and constant connectivity brought us comfort and accessibility. We can connect with anyone in the world with a push of a button or touch of a screen or just by saying their name. This is a great facility that we are blessed with that perhaps our ancestors never dreamed of. However, ironically, this digital over-connectedness is disconnecting us from ourselves and others and what is truly important in life.

There is a principle in quantum mechanics called Heisenberg's uncertainty principle. This principle, which is a fundamental principle in quantum mechanics, states that we cannot determine the position and the momentum—which is mass times velocity— of a particle simultaneously with precision. This means that the more accurately we can determine the position of a particle, the less accurately we will know the momentum of that particle, and vice versa.

This concept of uncertainty is applicable to our day-to-day life. When we go through the moments of our lives at higher speed, we will experience those moments with lower attention. We pass through them without really noticing them. As speed increases, attention decreases.

This is what I call *speed-attention uncertainty*. To increase our attention, we need to lower our speed. I first learned this lesson from a calligraphy master when I was nine years old.

My parents sent me to a calligraphy class to learn Persian calligraphy from a well-known calligraphy master. It turned out that I liked this art from the beginning.

Persian calligraphy is written with a special kind of pen carved from a unique type of reed using a particular type of ink.

The letters of the Persian alphabet, similar to those of the Arabic alphabet, create words with curved, soft shapes. Creating shape of the letters and words requires just the right turning of the wrist and movement of the hand. It takes years of practice to get the elegant proportions correct. It takes many more years to master the art.

But this is the technical part. The creative part of Persian calligraphy is like choreography but instead of putting movement together the calligrapher puts letters and words together to create a beautiful and balanced work of art. Most alphabets in Persian calligraphy can be written in a longer or a shorter form, and some words and alphabets can be written in different shapes. Deciding the shape of each word in a line requires another level of mastery.

Two months after I started attending the calligraphy class, my teacher told my father that he was impressed with my progress. I still remember the smile that came over my face when I heard this.

I enjoyed the classes so much, I looked forward to them every week. Not only for calligraphy but for spending time with my teacher. I realize now that I learned many lessons that had a great impact on my life from my calligraphy teacher that were far more important than calligraphy itself.

One of the things that he taught me was that in order to increase my attention, I needed to slow down.

When I was first learning calligraphy from him, I'd pay attention and write each word slowly to be able to create the shapes.

> By living with higher attention and increased concentration, we connect with the moments in our lives on a deeper level. We connect with life more.

However, after a few months when I'd learned the shapes, I wrote the words more quickly. This caused my progress to slow. He realized what was going on and one day he told me that writing slower helps you pay more attention and create the shapes better. Even though at that time I didn't understand the depth of this lesson, I felt he was telling me something important. I never forgot my calligraphy teacher's words.

Almost three decades later, they became the basis of *speed-attention uncertainty*: to increase attention, slow down.

Even in his sixties, having written calligraphy for almost his whole life, my teacher still wrote slowly and with full concentration. I now think perhaps calligraphy was a tool for him to remain in a focused and peaceful state of mind. There was a certain peaceful vibration around him and in his classroom that attracted me, like a magnet. Remembering the sound of my teacher's pen sliding over the glossy paper when he was writing calligraphy takes me right back to that peaceful space.

By living with higher attention and increased concentration, we connect with the moments in our lives on a deeper level. We connect with life more.

The speed and overstimulation of modern life makes this increasingly difficult. It leaves us less and less time for ourselves and for *living* our lives. We pass through each moment so hastily that we miss the essence of life that is hidden in each moment. We are partially present or sometimes hardly present in the moments of our life that are the only reality that we have.

Hence, we leave them un-lived, lost in the memories of the past or the worries of future.

We miss life because we are not *here* to live it. We are somewhere over *there*—in the past or in the future—but not here. Our restless minds are wandering most of the time, visiting everywhere but where we are here now.

As a result, our minds are racing, running after an imaginary happiness that is escaping from us hiding itself in the next new goal, in the next shiny thing, in the next moment, but not here in this moment where is the only place we have ever lived. Happiness, contentment, even relaxation turns into a goal rather than a state of being.

Think of it this way: The highway of the modern mind is heavy with traffic. Thoughts fly up and down the lanes. Just as on the road, the more cars clogging the highway, the less efficiently they travel. Fewer cars means more space between each automobile and more efficient travel.

We need more space in our minds.

Not enough space leads to stress.

Stress and the Overstimulation of the Fight-or-Flight Response

Because of our busy, overstimulated lives, our stress response, called the fight-or-flight response, is "on" most of the time. This creates a problem. The fight-or-flight response is a survival function that helped our ancestors survive as a human species. In times of danger, it should kick on to prepare the body to fight or flee a danger or threat.

When our ancestors saw a tiger in the wild, the flight-or-flight response would be triggered, slowing down all secondary functions, such as digestion, so the body could direct all of its energy to the muscles so it could either fight the tiger or run away from it. In this time of urgency, the body is temporarily out of balance. Once the danger is over, the body shifts gears again, returning to balance and repair-and-grow mode, also known as healing mode.

> We miss life because we are not *here* to live it. We are somewhere over *there*—in the past or in the future—but not here. Our restless minds are wandering most of the time, visiting everywhere but where we are here now.

The fight-or-flight response is essential in times of danger. But not all the time.

Today we are living in a new world with an old brain. This modern world overstimulates the fight-or-flight response, activating it so frequently that we are living in this survival mode almost all the time. Every time we feel stressed—whether it is from being stuck in a traffic jam, seeing a pile of emails in our inbox, or swerving to avoid an oncoming car—the same fight-or-flight mechanism is activated.

We hardly shift gears to healing mode. This leads to imbalance in the nervous system and entire body.

Under the grip of fight-or-flight, the way we see, think, perceive, feel, and behave are all affected.

In addition, maintaining fight or flight for an extended period requires a lot of energy and depletes the body's limited resources, making it much harder for it to function optimally. This effect negatively impacts our heart rate, digestion, immune system, and sleep. It also reduces our productivity, creativity, and decision-making. This overactive stress response can lead to anxiety, depression, and burn out.

Cell biologist Dr. Bruce Lipton writes in his book *The Biology of Belief,* "Almost every major illness that people acquire has been linked to chronic stress."[1]

What is significant is that the human brain cannot distinguish between real danger or an imagined one. We can trigger the stress response merely by our thoughts. We can relive our unwanted past experiences over and over again and get stressed out by rethinking about them in the now. Or we can anticipate an unwanted event in the future and live an imagined danger that never existed and may never exist.

> The human brain cannot distinguish between real danger or an imagined one. We can trigger the stress response merely by our thoughts.

When our wandering mind randomly brings up a memory from the past, it is usually a sad memory, not a happy one. And if it slips into the future, it brings the worries and the anticipation of what might go wrong. All of these negative thoughts are perceived by our brain as a threat to our survival.

The fact that we can create stress by our thoughts puts a significant amount of responsibility on us. It means we play a role in the stress response in our body.

Our Thoughts Can Create or Eliminate Stress

The word *stress* is a term in physics that has been used for centuries to express the internal forces in a material as the reaction to the external forces applied to that material. It was used for the first time in the medical domain by Dr. Hans Selye and popularized in 1950s to describe "the non-specific response of the organism to any pressure or demand."

> Our thoughts can create stress or eliminate it. It is essential to be aware of our thoughts and to be in charge of our mind to direct it towards choosing the positive thoughts rather than the negative ones.

Extensive studies over the past few decades show that we have a role to play in this response. The highlight of the outcome is what Dr. Jon Kabat-Zinn, professor emeritus of medicine at the University of Massachusetts Medical School, writes in his book *Full Catastrophe Living*, to summarize studies by Dr. Martin Seligman, who promoted Positive Psychology as a field of scientific study: "[I]t is not the potential stressor itself but how you perceive it and then how you handle it that will determine whether or not it will lead to stress."[2]

How we perceive the stressor, what meaning we give to it and how we respond to it, defines the effect the stressor will have on our mind and our body. What happens in our mind and our brain affects this response.

This emphasizes the importance of our mind and our thoughts on our well-being and the quality of our life.

Our thoughts can create stress or eliminate it.

It is essential to be aware of our thoughts and to be in charge of our mind to direct it towards choosing the positive thoughts rather than the negative ones.

The Focus Switch Model

At every moment we have a choice. We can choose to take a pause, tap into our wisdom, and decide *what to focus on*. Where we put our focus determines how we live our life. Where we put our focus, on positive or negative thoughts, determines whether we are in survival mode or healing mode.

Two main parts of the brain tare in competition for resources. (*i*) One is the amygdala, the ancient part of the brain. It is the brain's fight-or-flight center and initiates the stress response in the body. This is the autopilot or survival mode of the brain. (*ii*) The second part is the prefrontal cortex, the most recently developed part of the brain responsible for higher cognitive functions, such as attention, learning, and decision making. This is the conscious part of our brain.

These two parts cannot be active at the same time. Depending on the state of our mind and the thoughts that we carry, one of these parts is *on* while the other one is *off* at each moment.

You can't be conscious and unconscious at the same time. You can't have your hands on the steering wheel of your car and not on the steering wheel at the

> At every moment we have a choice. We can choose to take a pause, tap into our wisdom, and decide *what to focus on*. Where we put our focus determines how we live our life.

same time. You can choose one of these options at each moment, like flipping a switch that turns one part of the brain on while automatically flipping the other part off.

This is where *the Focus Switch Model* comes in. We can switch from autopilot mode to conscious mode by using our ability to focus and choosing to focus on positive thoughts and the positive aspects of life.

And the more energy and time we spend focused on the positive, the more positivity grows while depriving negativity of energy and shrinking it.

When we are in a survival or autopilot mode, we see ourselves as separate from the rest of the world and we see the world as potential danger; whereas when we are in conscious mode, we see ourselves as part of something bigger and supportive.

Imagine the thoughts in your mind water two different pots of plants. The positive thoughts water one plant while the negative thoughts water the other. With each thought you pour a drop of water on one of these pots. At each moment you have a choice which plant to nurture. In fact, at each moment you are watering one of these pots. The plant you water more frequently will grow while the other one will wither.

The parts of our brains wither if we don't use them frequently. This is why you've heard you should "use it or lose it."

There is a law in neuroscience, called the Hebb's law, which states "neurons that fire together wire together." This is the scientific way of saying that what we put our attention on will grow.

By watering the autopilot or survival part of the brain, we support it to make us feel more anxious and stressed. While we're watering the survival part of the brain, we're depriving the conscious part of water and it withers. As a result, our concentration, decision-making skills, and problem-solving ability become weaker.

How you function as a human being is determined by which of these modes you are in. The decisions that you make when you are in a state of fear and frustration, autopilot mode, are different from the decisions that you make when you are in a state of love and gratitude, conscious mode.

When we are in a survival or autopilot mode, we see ourselves as separate from the rest of the world and we see the world as potential danger; whereas when we are in conscious mode, we see ourselves as part of something bigger and supportive.

In survival mode, we perceive the world as competition. In conscious mode, we perceive the world as collaboration. We can't relax when we are in competition; we must strive to win. A collaboration, on the other hand, is comforting and reassuring; we can relax, support, and thrive together.

Both the survival and conscious modes are needed. But when the survival mode is overactive, it takes the mind out of balance.

> Both the survival and conscious modes are needed. But when the survival mode is overactive, it takes the mind out of balance. And an out-of-balance mind leads to an out-of-balance body. We have a role to play in how balanced our mind *and* body are.

And an out-of-balance mind leads to an out-of-balance body. We have a role to play in how balanced our mind *and* body are.

The thoughts you carry in your mind affect your body too. The mind is not separate from the body. The mind and the body are connected.

The Mind-Body Connection

Our body is a chemical soup and we are the chef; our mind is our tool and our thoughts are our ingredients. Our mind can significantly influence the chemical environment in our body and promote healing or prevent it, depending on how we use our mind and where we put our focus.

Our thoughts are *not* empty quantities with no impact. They use up the energy and the nutrition in our brain. Thoughts are associated with chemical reactions in our body. Each thought is translated into the body as an emotion. When you think a thought such as "I am loved" or "I am not loved," you feel different. Your thoughts are manifested in your body through the chemicals they trigger, ones that can cause happiness and calm or anxiety and tension.

> Our thoughts are *not* empty quantities with no impact. They use up the energy and the nutrition in our brain. Thoughts are associated with chemical reactions in our body. Each thought is translated into the body as an emotion.

Your body's capacity for healing depends on the chemical environment that you create in your body. Your state of mind and what you focus on determines the chemical environment in your body. Your mind has much more influence over your body than you can imagine.

It is important to understand that the thoughts in your mind may not be real, but the emotion that they create—the chemicals in your body—*are* real. We have the ability to think any thought we want whether it is true or not. When someone thinks "I am not loved," this thought may arise out of a fear of not being enough or a misinterpretation of a past event, or it may not have any solid basis at all. The source of the thought does not remove its effect on the body and the chemicals and the emotions that it generates.

Unreal thoughts create real emotions. We have the power to generate a real emotion from an unreal thought. In fact, most of our thoughts are not real. They are based on our memories of the past that are not real in the

> The thoughts in your mind may not be real, but the emotion that they create—the chemicals in your body—are real.

present moment where we live or based on our imagination about tomorrow that are not real yet or may never become real. The thoughts you think consciously or automatically define which messages are sent to your body and which types of chemicals are produced. And that is why it is important to be conscious of the present moment and to perceive what is happening in it.

We cannot separate ourselves from our life experiences. We participate in creating them by the thoughts that we carry in our mind and the meaning that we give to events.

According to quantum mechanics, the observer cannot be separated from the observed. The observer and the observed together create the experience of observation. We are an inseparable part of the realities that we perceive. Events (the observed) are not our realities. Together with our observations—how we receive them and how we interpret them—they become our realities. In other words, our realities depend on us.

This is liberating. If your thoughts participate in creating your life, then you can change your life experiences by changing your thoughts. This is a great responsibility. You need to check every thought that you carry in your mind, whether you are carrying them consciously or unconsciously, and choose to hold onto the thoughts that are life affirming and help you grow and thrive and let go of the thoughts that are making you shrink. Growth is a natural part of being *alive*. A living plant is a growing plant. Once a plant's growth stops, it starts to wither.

> We cannot separate ourselves from our life experiences. We participate in creating them by the thoughts that we carry in our mind and the meaning that we give to events. We are an inseparable part of the realities that we perceive.

We have choice. We can choose which thoughts to think and focus on.

We have this superpower. Now, we must strengthen this ability by understanding how our mind works and learning how to turn on the conscious mode so that we can consciously choose our thoughts—and consciously choose *life-affirming* thoughts.

This is why focus, the third pillar, plays such an outsized part in our lives. Focus is the switch that turns on conscious mode and turns off survival mode. The pillar of focus together with the two pillars of pause and wisdom makes life more stable. By taking a pause, we provide space to our mind to focus. And with wisdom, we consciously decide what to focus on.

We need focus to thrive in this fast-paced life. Otherwise, we will be limited to living in survival mode, unable to heal, thrive, and grow. Unable to unlock our best life.

The Role of Meditation

Masters of wisdom have known the importance of focus for thousands of years. They have studied the human mind intensively and created many techniques to develop the mind's ability to focus.

One of the most efficient methods to develop focus is meditation.

Meditation is a scientific process, a method of training the mind to focus. The object of the mind's focus may vary. You may focus on your breath or a sound, thought, or image. The act of focus is the common denominator.

Scientific research has shown the positive effects of meditation on physical, emotional, and mental health. Meditation improves focus, memory, creativity, learning ability, empathy, and sleep and reduces stress, and anxiety.[2,3,4,5] Meditation also reduces pain,[6] improves immune function[7] and promotes healing. These are just a few of its many benefits.

Meditation is a skill. And like any other skill, the more you practice, the more you will experience its benefits.

> If your thoughts participate in creating your life, then you can change your life experiences by changing your thoughts.

Meditation is not a religious practice. Anyone, regardless of their religious beliefs, can adopt the techniques of meditation to exercise their mind to become more fit and focused, the same way anyone can use any exercise for the body to make their body stronger and healthier.

But meditation includes more than exercises of focus. It is also about wisdom, knowing which thoughts to focus on and how to perceive yourself and the world around you to co-create your reality. Co-create because, remember, what we call our realities are created by the observed and the observer together.

Do you want to have positive thoughts that make you grow or do you want to have negative thoughts that make you shrink?

Meditation trains the mind to focus on the thoughts you want and strengthens its ability to hold onto those thoughts. Without this training, the brain is easily distracted and switches to autopilot mode.

We now know meditation changes the structure of the brain. There is a large body of scientific research that shows how meditation alters the physical brain structures of people who meditate compared to those who don't meditate.

Dr. Richard Davidson, professor of psychology and psychiatry at the University of Wisconsin–Madison and best known for his groundbreaking work studying emotion and the brain, says, "What we found is that the trained mind, or brain, is physically different from the untrained one."

Using magnetic resonance imaging (MRI) scans of experienced meditators, Dr. Sara Lazar and her research team from Harvard Medical School and Massachusetts General Hospital showed that long-term meditation correlates with thickening of the brain regions associated with attention, sensory processing, and interoception, how we experience bodily sensations.[8]

They also studied the physical impact on individuals who began practicing meditation for the first time. Within eight weeks of their first session, participants had increased their gray matter in areas of the brain associated with learning and memory, self-awareness, compassion, and introspection.[9]

In addition to an increase in gray matter in these parts of the brain, the researchers found a decrease in gray matter in the amygdala, the part of the brain responsible for stress, fear, and anxiety. Their research showed that decreased gray matter in the amygdala correlates with lower stress.[10]

These findings show the importance of focus and its effect on our brain, our well-being, and our life.

While the strategies in part 2 will not teach you formal practices of meditation, they were inspired by meditation techniques and will strengthen your mind's ability to focus. They will gradually train your brain to spend more time in conscious mode, focused on the thoughts you choose, rather than in survival mode.

Heal Your Mind, Heal Your Life

Developing focus so you are able to hold on to positive thoughts is the most loving thing you can do for yourself, for the people you love, and for the rest of the world. And it is the wisest thing you can do to heal physical, mental, and emotional pain, such as stress, anxiety, depression, low self-esteem, resentment, and lack of self-love and unlock your best life.

It is especially critical to keep your mind focused on positive thoughts when you are physically sick or in pain. In times of difficulty, our mind naturally tends to focus on what is going wrong and on the negative in general. It is in such times, that focusing on positive thoughts can make a significant difference in our life experience.

In the case of chronic illnesses, it is important to know that the body can heal itself. But you need to support your body's healing by providing the right conditions for it. Your thoughts affect your body's chemistry. Your body cannot heal itself as long as your stress response is triggered and you are living in survival mode. In order to provide your body with a healing environment, you need to make sure you spend as much time as possible in conscious mode, focused on positive thoughts.

When you focus on positive thoughts, you create a happy mind and your body produces chemicals that promote a feeling of happiness. These chemicals support the body's natural ability to heal. Swami Rama, one of the greatest masters of twentieth century and founder of the Himalayan Institute, writes in his book *Happiness Is Your Creation*, "A happy mind is the source of all healing powers."[11]

He goes on to write, "Happiness is a virtue of a positive mind, while pain is the fruit of a negative mind. By cultivating a positive mind, you can be happy; and by holding on to a negative mind, you can be miserable."

The following strategies will help you cultivate a positive mind.

Part Two

7 Simple Strategies to Increase Focus, Heal Your Pain, and Unlock Your Best Life

CHAPTER 3

REFINE YOUR LIMITING BELIEFS

WHEN I FIRST learned that I had Lyme disease and the doctor shared all the information he knew about it, I believed certain things that greatly influenced my journey to healing in a negative way. I trusted that the information he shared were facts and I did not question them. I was not careful about what I let into my mind. That was a mistake that I paid for in different ways in the months to come and made my path to recovery more challenging than it could have been.

At the time, I was already using many strategies every day to promote the production of healing chemicals in my body. These strategies were supporting my healing immensely but a limiting belief was holding me back. By holding on to this limiting belief, I was unknowingly slowing my journey to recovery.

That day in the doctor's office, I believed that the bacteria causing this disease know their survival tricks so well that my body would be *un*able to eradicate them. I believed that only a select few have the genes to fight these bacteria and I am one of the unlucky ones who don't have them. I believed that, at most, I could get the bacteria under control, but I could never get rid of them completely. I believed that fighting these bacteria is a long arduous path that I would have to walk whether I wanted to or not.

For two days after learning my diagnosis, I was in a state of shock. I was having a hard time accepting that all my plans, all the things that I wished to do, would be on hold for an uncertain amount of time. I didn't have to accept this thought—it was just an idea, not reality—but fear paralyzed my thinking and I believed I had fallen into a situation with no way out.

On the third day, I had a moment of realization: "I can heal and the intelligence that is inseparable from my existence is supporting me, as it always is." With this thought, my perception of this experience and what it could mean in my life shifted.

With this shift, a new door opened in my mind, a door that opened a path and a promise to a good outcome from all of this. I made a critical decision at that moment. I decided to turn this disease into a positive event in my life by making it a springboard for my growth.

I started to keep my focus on the positives and my best future instead of on temporary pain and discomfort and the potential scary future with this disease. Consciously holding the positives in my mind helped me go through this time gracefully and peacefully and supported my body's healing.

However, that limiting belief lingered and it didn't occur to me to question my belief that my body could only heal the damage caused by the bacteria but not defeat them. Even after my moment of realization, I still carelessly accepted this as a fact: my body needed outside intervention to kill the bacteria for it.

I thought of it like this: my body is my house and some invaders broke into it, breaking furniture and creating a mess. My body is capable of fixing the furniture and cleaning up the mess. And, with the help of meditation and my other strategies, I can provide the materials and conditions for it to do the fixing and the cleaning. But my body cannot throw the burglars out. It needs an outsider, a police officer or guard to toss them out and prevent them from coming back.

Believing my body's limitations made me more vulnerable to the bacteria and limited my power to protect my house from the invaders.

One year after my initial diagnosis, when I had been going through treatment for nine months, I was feeling better and my symptoms were improving overall but progress had not been smooth. At no point did I think my doctor and I had these bacteria under control for good.

Eventually, my progress reached a plateau. The doctor suggested I take a new test that would measure my body's capacity to heal, among many other markers. I took the test and two days later the doctor showed me the results.

"I want to show you something very interesting," he said. "The results show that your body has an excellent capacity to heal itself. In fact, your test results are much better than mine!"

As the doctor spoke, he pointed to a graph charting my test results on a monitor. I couldn't believe my eyes. There it was, the blue bar indicating my body's healing power was in the highest range for healing capacity.

Seeing that opened a door in my mind that allowed light to come flooding through, filling me.

The doctor continued, "Other patients' bodies don't have a very good capacity to heal and they need treatment. I think the treatments we are doing here don't work well for you because we do a little treatment and it helps your body, and your body can do the rest and heal itself. But then we push it off balance again by continuing the treatment. These treatments are too aggressive for your body. Instead, I think you should do some very gentle treatments that just support your body's healing."

I agreed, and after I finished the two sessions remaining of the protocol I had already started, I did not go back to the clinic again. I didn't need to.

Seeing those test results changed the way I saw my body. No longer was it in need of help. No longer was it dependent on outside treatments to prevent the bacteria from spreading. Now, I trusted that my body was perfectly capable of healing itself and getting rid of these bacteria on its own.

Although I stopped treatments, my health improved quickly and consistently.

Once my belief shifted from "my body cannot fight these bacteria" to "my body has the capacity to protect itself and heal itself," everything changed. My body was already doing its job extremely well, but by unconsciously holding on to one limiting belief I was slowing down its progress.

My new belief was supportive and empowering.

This is how powerful belief is.

The Power of Beliefs

Our beliefs play a significant role in our life. Positive thoughts and life-supporting beliefs help us grow and thrive while negative thoughts and limiting beliefs make us shrink.

Examples of limiting beliefs include the following:

> I'm not good enough.
> I'm not worthy.
> I can't do it.
> I was never good at this.
> I don't deserve it.
> No one loves me.
> I'm too old (young, tall, overweight, etc.).
> I don't have any talents.
> I'm not smart (strong, beautiful, talented, etc.) enough.
> I don't have enough resources (knowledge, money, etc.)

We all have some unconscious limiting beliefs and these beliefs influence our perceptions, feelings, behaviors, and health. They influence the way we live and experience life. As these beliefs are unconscious, we are not aware of them. But being unaware of them doesn't change their influence. And their influence over every aspect of our lives is significant.

Our mind has a conscious part and a subconscious part. The conscious mind works based on

> Our beliefs play a significant role in our life. Positive thoughts and life-supporting beliefs help us grow and thrive while negative thoughts and limiting beliefs make us shrink.

logic and reasoning and makes decisions. It is also the creative mind that holds our wishes and desires. With all its vastness, the conscious mind accounts for only about 5 percent of our mind.[12]

The other 95 percent of the mind is the subconscious mind that stores all our past experiences and the learned patterns and conditionings those experiences taught us.

The subconscious mind handles everything that seems to happen automatically. Most of our actions throughout the day are well-learned patterns maintained by our subconscious mind. Think of the actions that you do the same way every day without seeming to think about them: getting out of bed, eating breakfast, brushing your teeth, walking out your front door, driving to work.

You don't need to be aware of these actions. They happen without being conscious of them. Once the mind learns something and it becomes a pattern, then the subconscious mind performs it very efficiently.

To test this, try to walk down a set of stairs consciously, at your normal pace, instead of in automatic mode. I must warn you: be very careful. There are many things to consciously consider. You need to position your feet on the narrow step in exactly the right place. A few inches off and you may fall down the step. Once you manage to put one foot on the step successfully, you now need to consciously repeat the process again and again. Are you moving at your usual speed or are these few steps taking you much longer?

After taking a few steps with conscious effort, take a few more automatically. Just walk down the steps as your body always does. Easy isn't it? You could even run down the steps without thinking about it; your feet know exactly where to go.

Now, switch back to conscious mode. Ah! The moment you think about what is required to run down the stairs, you will find it almost impossible and may even fall.

Once your subconscious mind learned how to navigate stairs, it is able to perform this difficult task effortlessly and automatically with perfect precision and efficiency. On the other hand, your conscious mind requires a lot of energy and effort to do it. Your subconscious mind makes your life easier by taking charge of the repetitive things that you do every day.

Our subconscious mind even has the capacity to walk us in our sleep. You have probably heard of sleepwalking. Sleepwalkers can get out of bed, walk to the kitchen, open the fridge, and eat the dessert that they didn't finish at dinner. They can even open the front door, leave the house, walk a few blocks, and then return home, without trouble finding the address or bumping into things. Sleepwalkers can do all this while they are asleep and without being aware they are doing it.

Like sleepwalkers, we are almost not aware of most of what we do during the day. That is how efficiently our subconscious mind works.

The subconscious mind is bigger and more powerful than the conscious mind. According to neuroscientist Dr. Herbert Zimmermann, we receive 11 million bits of sensory information per second, out of which we consciously process only around 40 bits.[13] The rest is processed unconsciously.

Most of our behaviors and patterns in life are run by the programs in our subconscious mind. And those programs were written in our subconscious mind during our childhood when our conscious mind hadn't evolved enough to analyze and choose

Most of our behaviors and patterns in life are run by the programs in our subconscious mind. And those programs were written in our subconscious mind during our childhood when our conscious mind hadn't evolved enough to analyze and choose what to believe and what to conclude about our environment and our experiences.

what to believe and what to conclude about our environment and our experiences.

Many of our beliefs about ourselves and the world are shaped before the age of seven. From ordinary day-to-day things—such as what and how to eat, what to wear and how to dress, how to speak and what to say—to our beliefs about who we are as an individual and what we are capable of, and our position in society and in the world are taught to us by our parents, teachers, and other mentors in the society.

These beliefs can shape our whole lives if we don't consciously check them and replace the limiting ones with empowering beliefs.

You Are the Fish in the Ocean with No Barrier

In 1873, zoologist Dr. Karl Möbius did an experiment on a fish that is relevant to humans and shows the effect of a learned limiting belief.

He put a large fish in a tank of water and divided the tank into two parts by inserting a glass wall in the middle. He then put the food (small prey fish) in the other section of the tank. Whenever the fish went for its prey, it hit the glass divider. It tried over and over again, but each time it crashed into the glass wall. It eventually gave up and never tried to go for the small fishes again. Even after the glass divider was removed and the small fishes were swimming next to him, the fish never attacked the small fishes and ate only the other foods Dr. Möbius gave it.

This experiment was repeated by other researchers later who allowed the large fishes starve to death by not giving them any food other than the small prey fish. Once the large fishes gave up, they never went for their prey again and died.

> We can become the conscious creators of our lives, using our conscious minds to observe the behaviors and beliefs coming from our subconscious minds and deciding to adopt different ones if they don't serve us.

Like the fishes in the experiment, we have limiting beliefs that prevent us from living a fulfilling life and from doing what we are capable of. They will continue to rule our lives if we don't question those beliefs.

Become a Conscious Creator

We can decide to function based on these automatic patterns and unchecked beliefs in our subconscious minds or we can consciously choose what we want to believe and how we want to behave.

We can become the conscious creators of our lives, using our conscious minds to observe the behaviors and beliefs coming from our subconscious minds and deciding to adopt different ones if they don't serve us. We don't have to be a victim of our subconscious minds running the show most of the time.

We have the ability to choose how to respond to our life circumstances and how we experience life. We can choose our thoughts, our beliefs, and our actions.

Ask yourself: Do you want to be a conscious creator or live by default, letting your subconscious fly the plane of your life on autopilot?

If you want to become a conscious creator (and I am sure that you do), take a closer look at your life to try to determine your limiting beliefs. Consider the areas of your life that displease you or aren't what you want them to be. Perhaps it's your job, family life, or self-esteem. It's likely you have limiting beliefs in that area. The good news is, you can consciously decide to replace them with empowering beliefs that support you in living a happy and fulfilling life.

When you want to achieve something, whether it is happiness, success, good health, wealth, or anything else, reflect: Do you believe you can achieve it? Do you believe you deserve it? Or, deep inside do you believe you cannot do it and/or don't deserve it? The latter, negative beliefs will block your way.

> We have the ability to choose how to respond to our life circumstances and how we experience life. We can choose our thoughts, our beliefs, and our actions.

If you think what you hope to attain is possible and you deserve it, you will make the effort to make it happen. When you think it is not possible or you don't deserve it, you may not even attempt to achieve it.

On May 6, 1954, Roger Bannister did something that was once said to be impossible. He ran a mile in less than 4 minutes—3:59.4 to be exact. At that time, scientists thought the human body had a limit and it could not break the 4-minute barrier. They thought an athlete could die trying to break it. But Bannister questioned this belief and broke the 4-minute barrier as well as this belief barrier.

Once Bannister changed this belief, the rest of the world also believed that it was possible and Bannister's record lasted for only forty-six days. Because forty-six days later, another athlete ran a mile in less than 4 minutes and even more rapidly than Bannister. Since then, athletes have been breaking the 4-minute-mile barrier and the record over and over again.

The body's limitation is in fact the mind's limitation. Once you change the belief in your mind, you will change your body's performance and your results in life, too.

The Placebo and Nocebo Effects

You can even heal your body when you believe that you can. In several studies, patients given fake medicine[14] or even fake surgery[15] got better just by believing that they were receiving a real treatment. This is called the *placebo effect*.

The opposite is true as well. Thinking positively, leads to a positive outcome. Thinking negatively, leads to a negative one. The latter is called the *nocebo effect*.

Just as the placebo effect can have a powerful impact on our life and our health, the nocebo effect can, too.

If you believe that you are going to heal, your positive attitude and empowering belief moves your body toward health. Similarly, if you believe that you are not going to heal, your negative attitude and belief will move your body toward disease.

This is how health care practitioners can have an even greater impact—positive or negative—on your body's ability to heal and your health overall. If you need to go to a practitioner, go with a belief that your body has the ability to heal itself and there is no physical condition that you cannot overcome. Hear the information that the doctor provides, but if they are pointing to negativity, don't accept negativity as reality.

> The body's limitation is in fact the mind's limitation. Once you change the belief in your mind, you will change your body's performance and your results in life, too.

Even people with the most severe, even terminal, diseases have been healed despite their doctor's prognosis.

An inspiring example of such a case is described in the book *Dying to Be Me*[16] by Anita Moorjani. In this book, Anita explains how she had been battling cancer when she fell into a coma and her organs started to shut down. She experienced a near death experience that revealed to her why she got cancer. She was given a choice whether to come back to her body or to die. She chose to come back. And her body started to rapidly heal after she came back from the coma and the near-death experience.

Such cases may be labeled as an exception, miracle, or spontaneous remission. However, there are no exceptions in the laws of nature. What we call a miracle or an exception happens within the laws of nature as well. But we don't know all the laws of nature and we cannot explain some phenomena, so we give them such labels.

Whenever physicists find an exception to a theory, they know that the theory is incomplete and they start looking for a more complete model that can include those exceptions or for a new model altogether.

Exceptions show us where we are going wrong. This is how science progresses. If physicists disregarded exceptions and held on to the flawed or incomplete theories, many great discoveries would have never happened.

There is no exception in the laws of nature.

> Disease in the body is a sign, a symptom, of an underlying root cause. It may be unresolved negative emotions, an unhealthy lifestyle or environment, or some other causes. If you find and fix the root cause, then you remove the blockage for healing and your body will do the rest according to its capacity.

Talking on a cell phone would seem like a miracle to people living a thousand years ago but now it's no big deal.

And still there are many things about the laws of nature that we have yet to discover. Better not to underestimate your body, a part of this powerful, yet unmapped, universe.

Disease in the body is a sign, a symptom, of an underlying root cause. It may be unresolved negative emotions, an unhealthy lifestyle or environment, or some other causes. If you find and fix the root cause, then you remove the blockage for healing and your body will do the rest according to its capacity. But never underestimate its capacity until you've found the real cause of the disease and removed that cause.

Our beliefs are powerful influences on our life. We should be very careful about what we let into our minds and what we believe.

We may think that we want to be happy, healthy, successful, loving, loved, etc. These are desires in the conscious mind. But if the beliefs in our subconscious mind are not in alignment with these desires, then the *unconscious* beliefs will determine our results in life.

When you believe you can heal your pain, whether physical, emotional, or mental, you can.

And you can replace limiting beliefs with empowering ones. The following technique, *Refine Your Limiting Beliefs*, will show you how to examine your beliefs and correct them if they are not supporting your growth and in alignment with your conscious intention.

The Benefits of the *Refine Your Limiting Beliefs* Technique

We all have limiting beliefs. If we leave them unchecked, they will prevent us from thriving and healing.

We may think that we want to be happy, healthy, successful, loving, loved, etc. These are desires in the conscious mind. But if the beliefs in our subconscious mind are not in alignment with these desires, then the *unconscious* beliefs will determine our results in life. Because the subconscious mind is more powerful than the conscious mind if we live on autopilot mode.

Our conscious mind can be in charge only when we are conscious, are thinking consciously, and acting consciously. That is why it is important to practice switching from the default mode to the conscious mode as often as you can. In the conscious mode you can check your beliefs.

We may become conscious for a moment and think that we want to be happy, healthy, successful, but when we go back to the default mode, the subconscious mind starts running the show again. The conscious mind is a powerful tool, but only when you are using this tool—only when you are conscious.

You have the power to be the conscious creator of your life.

You can rewrite your beliefs. You can reprogram your mind. You can decide which beliefs to hold on to and which ones to replace. No matter what your beliefs are and how they are limiting your life, you can change them at every moment in your life.

Life is too precious to waste on limiting beliefs.

If we want to grow and expand, heal our pain, and unlock our best lives, we must correct our beliefs.

That's exactly what the Refine Your Limiting Beliefs technique will help you to do. This simple technique will show you how to

- find your 4-minute barriers and break them, just as Roger Bannister did;
- become aware of the beliefs, the invisible forces, that are influencing the direction of your life and your behaviors;
- look carefully to see if those beliefs are serving you or not; and
- replace limiting beliefs that do not work for you with empowering beliefs that do.

How to Do the *Refine Your Limiting Beliefs* Technique

To check your beliefs and modify the limiting ones, examine your life now. Think of an area of your life that you wish to improve or a pain that you want to heal. Look at where you have struggle, challenge, or pain in your life. Follow these steps:

Step 1: *Identify your limiting beliefs.*

Notice what you say to yourself about yourself in that area. Observe your thoughts and beliefs. Do you believe on some level that you deserve to have this problem, or do you believe you deserve the best possible outcome in that area? Do you believe that you can heal this aspect of your life?

Look at the situation from different angles and try to bring out your beliefs in that area.

For example, if you have a health issue: Do you believe that your body can heal itself? Or do you believe that your body is weak? Do you feel any guilt that you think makes you deserve this health issue? Or do you feel you deserve to be completely healthy? Do you believe that you can do simple things to help your healing? Or do you believe that there is nothing you can do?

Observe carefully and look deeply to see what you really think about this health issue, how you really want your health to be, and how you see your ability to heal it.

As another example, if you want to follow your dream and become a musician, an entrepreneur, an Olympic champion, a chef, an author, or anything that is your dream, and you find that something is stopping you from following this dream: Do you believe that you can do it or that you can't? Do you believe that you deserve it or that you don't deserve it? Do you believe that you are smart enough, strong enough, persistent enough, talented enough, and so forth, to achieve your dream, or do you believe you are not enough?

If you are unable to identify your limiting beliefs in this way, try a different approach. Think: What is the most empowering belief I could have? For example, I am worthy, I am lovable, I deserve it, I can do it, I love myself. And then say this empowering belief as loud as you can.

If you find that you can't say it without hesitation and as loud as you can, then it might be because you don't believe in this empowering belief. You've just identified a limiting belief.

Take your time identifying limiting beliefs. Keep searching until you find the ones unconsciously influencing your life. There is no judgment here about your beliefs. It is a practice of educating yourself about the deeper dimensions of your thoughts and correcting the ones that are not supporting you.

If you are struggling to identify a limiting belief, turn to table 3.1 on page 68 for some additional ideas.

Step 2: *Write down your limiting beliefs.*

Once you have identified your limiting beliefs, list them in the left column on table 3.2 on page 69.

Step 3: *Write down the corresponding empowering beliefs.*

Then, on the right-hand side of the table, next to each limiting belief, write down its opposite, an empowering belief. Empowering beliefs support what you truly desire.

What do you need to believe in order to create your best future? Write that.

Look at the table 3.1 for some examples of limiting beliefs and corresponding empowering ones.

Step 4: *Decide to choose the empowering beliefs rather than the limiting ones.*

Is the outcome that you desire worth changing your belief from the limiting belief on the left side of the table to the empowering belief on the right side? If you feel that it is worth it, then decide that from this point onward you are going to live according to the empowering belief.

Step 5: *Practice your empowering belief.*

Whenever you catch yourself saying the limiting belief, correct yourself immediately and repeat the empowering belief. Say it once or repeat it as many times as you want. Do this until the empowering belief becomes the default belief in your mind.

If you find that you are usually not conscious of what you say to yourself, then (1) pick the limiting belief that is most important for you to work on, (2) set a time once or a few times a day to specifically remind yourself of your new empowering belief to replace this limiting one. For example, every morning, before your start your day, repeat your empowering belief, in your mind or say it out loud. You can even sing your new empowering belief, to really help make it stick.

The more often and enthusiastically you repeat your new empowering belief, the quicker you will replace the corresponding limiting belief.

The *Refine Your Limiting Beliefs* Technique in Action

I first met Jane at one of my talks about happiness in Sydney and she signed up for my G.R.O.W. program to grow her mind and grow her life. During the program, she acknowledged that she wanted to feel better about her body. The first thing she wanted to do was lose weight.

When she started to examine her beliefs about her weight, she quickly identified a limiting belief: If I eat, I'll get fat. Her mother had always told Jane and her two sisters to eat less because everyone is fat in their family and they would inevitably get fat, too. All her life, Jane deprived herself of her favorite foods and desserts because she feared they would make her fat. Even so, she was unhappy about the extra pounds she carried.

I encouraged Jane to consider how her mother's words may be contributing to her relationship with food. She agreed to question her belief and become more conscious of her eating behavior and food choices to see how her belief about food was affecting how she approached eating.

When she became conscious of how she ate, Jane noticed that she often avoided main meals, but because she was always hungry, she snacked all day, and not on healthy snacks most of the time.

Jane identified an empowering belief to replace the limiting one: I can enjoy food without gaining weight. Her next steps were to eat main meals instead of snacking all day and enjoy her meals by eating her favorite foods. Jane started to see food as nutrients for her body rather than extra weight and became more conscious of making healthy food

> Healing your life and unlocking your highest potential can sometimes be as easy as changing your beliefs about them and consciously choosing to live according to those empowering beliefs moment by moment.

choices. It was easy to convince Jane of the health benefits of replacing fatty, sugary snacks with a proper meal.

It took Jane almost a month for her new empowering belief to stick. Soon she noticed that her relationship with food was changing. She was allowing herself to *enjoy* eating and making conscious choices about the food she eats. She replaced "fear" of eating with "joy" of eating.

Two months after she started this practice, she not only didn't gain weight but instead started losing weight. Seeing this result, Jane realized how her previous limiting belief had contributed to her negative relationship with food and her weight. According to Jane, it felt better to enjoy herself instead of restricting herself.

Another six months passed and Jane was eating more than before, including her favorite desserts (occasionally), and still losing weight. She continued to *enjoy* her meals and choose foods to nourish her body.

She shared, "All my adult life, I wished I could eat a whole brownie and not gain weight. And now, I'm eating my favorite desserts and not only am I not gaining weight; I'm losing weight. And I have more energy."

One year later, Jane reached her ideal weight without restricting her food and savoring it more than before. This experience has built Jane's confidence. Now she knows she can become conscious of a limiting belief, take the steps necessary to change it, and improve her life. She's started to examine her other limiting beliefs as well.

The Significance of the *Refine Your Limiting Beliefs* Technique

Healing your life and unlocking your highest potential can sometimes be as easy as changing your beliefs about them and consciously choosing to live according to those empowering beliefs moment by moment.

This one life is too precious to waste because of a few limiting beliefs. It is worth challenging your limiting beliefs and choosing to replace them with empowering ones, even if it takes some work and effort to change old thought and behavior patterns.

You may want to hold on to your limiting beliefs because it is more convenient to hold on to what you know than risk the discomfort of adapting to a new pattern or lifestyle. But a new life based on empowering beliefs is more fulfilling and a better use of your precious life.

At the end of your life, you don't want to look back and regret postponing joy because you postponed changing your limiting beliefs and transforming your life.

If you don't start changing those limiting beliefs, you are going to live a life that is less than what you truly deserve. It is *always* worth the effort.

Do not let events or others define who you are. Believe that you deserve the best, you deserve to be happy, healthy, wealthy, loved, free.

We are here to grow. And the extent to which we grow is defined by the extent of the glass wall that we build in our mind.

There is no limit to your growth and there is no limit to your potential if there is no limit in your mind.

Table 3.1 Examples of Limiting Beliefs and the Empowering Beliefs to Replace Them

Limiting belief	Empowering belief
I'm not worthy.	I am worthy.
I can't do it.	I can do it.
I was never good at this.	I can become better at it with practice.
I don't deserve it.	I deserve it.
Nobody loves me.	I love myself.
I'm too old.	It's never late to follow my dreams.
I don't have any talents.	I am good at […].
I'm not smart enough.	I can learn whatever is needed.
I am not strong enough.	I am strong.
I don't have enough resources.	There are enough resources out there.
I'm not attractive.	I am beautiful just the way I am.
I am sick.	I am healthy.
It's her fault.	I'm in charge of my own life.
I don't know how to do it.	I will learn the skills necessary.

Table 3.2 List Your Limiting Beliefs and Replace Them with New, Empowering Beliefs

Limiting belief	Empowering belief

CHAPTER 4

CREATE MINDFUL DISTRACTION

IN NOVEMBER 2017, I started experimenting with a new simple practice I could do throughout my day to bring me back to the present moment and remind myself of what a gift my life is.

For several months, I had been paying attention to how often during the day I could remember to bring myself into the present moment and keeping track of how long I could stay in the moment each time. I was surprised to realize that I only remembered a few times each day to become fully present and I could only hold my full attention for a few seconds before my mind got distracted. When I felt discomfort in my body or in my mind, my mind became distracted more easily.

I knew the importance of being in the present moment and how much keeping my focus on it helps me in every way, especially easing the discomfort in my body and mind that was growing more intense. I needed to find a way to remain more present throughout the day. By November, I had come up with a practice to train my mind to come back to the present moment over and over during the day.

I'd set the alarm on my phone to go off each hour from the time I woke up until the time I went to bed to remind me to bring my attention back to the present moment and to appreciate my life.

On the first day, I was sitting in my room working on my laptop. The alarm on my phone went off.

The phone was on a bookshelf a few steps away. I got up, went to my phone, and turned it off. Then I closed my eyes and took a deep breath while paying close attention to my breath and its value. Since birth, this simple humble breath has been my loyal companion. It is life itself. Taking that breath in I felt a breeze of life enter me, nourishing my body and my soul.

I breathed out this breath with a feeling of gratitude for the life it provided at this moment and felt grateful for being alive and the joy it brings. I spent a few more seconds breathing in and out with full attention.

When I opened my eyes, the daylight looked brighter, the plants in the room looked more vibrant, and the trees outside my window looked more alive. They were as they were a moment before, but I had become more attentive and open to my surroundings. By giving a moment of attention to my breathing, I felt a deeper sense of being alive and a calmer sense of *be*-ing.

One hour later, the same practice, the same breath, the same attention, and the same feeling.

In the moment that I was fully present with my breath and the gift of life, discomfort would loosen its grip from my mind and my body.

Be Mindful of Distractions

This practice became one of my most dependable strategies to stay calm, happy, and focused during the challenges of the Lyme disease treatments. It significantly eased my pain. But, more important, it brought my attention to the present moment more frequently and helped to anchor me in it more often.

This simple practice changed the nature of my relationship with my experience of life throughout the day. Reminding myself of the preciousness of each breath and the gift of life at least once an hour every day made me more aware of the value of this gift in general. I found myself compelled to address this topic in my articles and speeches about living a happy and stress-free life.

I was reaping great benefits from this practice. It was easy to follow and it took almost no time. But sometimes the alarm would go off at an inconvenient time, like when I was in the middle of a conversation or meeting. At those times I would excuse myself at that moment to turn off the alarm while becoming more conscious of my breath during the conversation.

A few times, the alarm went off just as I'd started my meditation practice. Early on, I had made a commitment to myself not to end my daily practice early. I promised to myself to take my meditation practices seriously and finish the practice without interruption once I sit for meditation. So when the alarm went off, I didn't want to stop my practice to get up and turn it off. I continued my meditation while the alarm kept ringing for fifteen minutes until it stopped by itself. And it was quite a nuisance, creating a distraction every time it rang.

But even in the moments where the alarm felt like a distraction, it still reminded me to be conscious of the present moment.

And that gave me the idea to use the distractions in our daily lives to our advantage. We can use the rings, buzzes, beeps, and dings from our cell phones and digital devices as reminders to become conscious of the present moment. The *Mindful Distraction*[17] technique was born.

Mindful Distraction is a technique and a concept that I created in 2018 to describe a simple practice to use distractions to our advantage.

Distraction

Distraction is a natural quality of an untrained mind. But in today's world we are facing distraction more than ever before. We are living in a digital age where all our digital devices—smartphones, laptops, tablets, etc.—and our social media feeds and digital ads are constantly trying to grab our attention in one way or another, and they are distracting us from where we are and what we do.

Electronic devices have brought us 24/7 connectivity and easy access to information, making our lives easier in many ways. We've gotten so used to the conveniences they've brought us that it seems impossible to live without these devices now.

However, our dependence on these gadgets comes at a significant cost. They disrupt one of the essential skills that we as human beings need to thrive in life: the ability to focus.

The near-continuous beeps, dings, rings, and buzzes coming from our devices to let us know we have a new email, text, or social media update make it hard to concentrate on anything for long. Bombarded with information all day long, from the time we wake up in the morning to the moment we go to bed at night, our brain is busier and more distracted than ever before. Our attention is fragmented. And the more these outside stimulants distract us, the more our brain becomes wired for distraction.

Every time we get distracted, our brain rewards us by producing dopamine, a chemical messenger in our brain that makes us feel good, because our brain loves novelty. And this trains our brain to want to be distracted again.

This is what neuroscientists call the "novelty bias." Our brain wants something new because it thinks there might be something better in the next new thing. Our brain is always searching for something else rather than what is here now. It runs ahead of us and wants to be in the next moment rather than the one we are in right now, and it encourages us to want to see the next new thing rather than wanting to see what is in front of us right now.

It's like the brain is hurrying us to run to the future rather than relaxing in the now. Have you noticed when you want to sit quietly, not fulfilling any task or doing one of the things in your to-do list, you feel bored? It feels uncomfortable to sit just for the sake of *being*, not doing anything. For some people it is unbearable to sit quietly without planning to do something or occupying their time and their mind with something in order to avoid the present moment they are in.

The modern world is full of distractions that feed this quality of the brain and train our mind to crave more distraction. Our brains are getting addicted to overstimulation. In fact, the more we get distracted, the more we get conditioned to want to be distracted. Eventually, we get to the point where we start distracting ourselves, no outside stimuli required.

Staying focused on one task is becoming a challenge for most people these days. According to Deloitte's *2017 Global Mobile*

Consumer Survey: US Edition, adults checked their phone on average fifty times a day in 2017.[18] We often feel a need to check our emails or social media feeds frequently to see if something is happening, even when we don't hear any notification sound.

Constant distraction is detrimental to our brains. It has a negative impact on our performance, productivity, and ability to focus, not to mention its negative influence on our relationships[19] and our sense of happiness.[20]

Moreover, frequent distraction decreases our attention span. A lower attention span means we are in survival or autopilot mode more often. This can result in stress, anxiety, depression, and burnout.

> Constant distraction is detrimental to our brains. It has a negative impact on our performance, productivity, and ability to focus, not to mention its negative influence on our relationships and our sense of happiness.

And there are more distractions to come. We may want to resist them, but entirely removing distractions in this fast-paced modern world is not realistic. In the future, artificial intelligence, robotics, and digital homes will create more and more distraction, making it even harder for us to disconnect from the outside world, take a pause, and connect with ourselves.

There is no doubt that technology makes our life easier. However, with any great discovery and advance in technology comes the responsibility of how to use them so that they benefit rather than harm us.

More than ever, we need to equip ourselves with the wisdom and tools to use the blessings of technology to our advantage so it does not disrupt our lives.

The Benefits of the *Mindful Distraction* Technique

There is one thing we can do to regain our attention and minimize the negative effects of distraction: consciously enhance our ability to pay attention.

Our ability to remain focused is one of the key factors that defines the quality of our lives and our level of happiness. The more we practice paying attention, the more we strengthen our ability to pay attention.

One of the best ways to enhance our attention is to practice mindfulness. Being mindful means being in the moment with full attention. Mindfulness, which is one of the branches of meditation, is an ancient technique and a scientific process that trains the mind to learn to be focused.

While distraction takes us away from where we are here and now, mindfulness trains our mind to remain in the moment we are currently in. Having a daily mindfulness practice is an effective way to slow down the mind and retain its focus.

> There is one thing we can do to regain our attention and minimize the negative effects of distraction: consciously enhance our ability to pay attention. Our ability to remain focused is one of the key factors that defines the quality of our lives and our level of happiness.

However, mindfulness is not only about doing an exercise for a few minutes a day. It is about staying mindful moment by moment as we go through our day. Every moment that we have mindful attention and focus counts. All these micro doses of mindfulness combine to strengthen our attention muscles.

If you step into a moment with full attention, even if it is just one moment, you are connecting with your conscious mode for that moment. You turn off survival mode and you become conscious. You feel calm and relaxed. This one moment of mindful attention affects the next moment and the one that comes after that and so on, until the effect wears off over time.

Mindful Distraction uses distractions in a positive way by seeing them as reminders to practice focus and become mindful for a moment. The very distractions that harm you are now benefiting you by helping you make a habit of paying attention. They become a trigger to create a moment of mindful attention.

If you bring yourself back to a moment of mindfulness over and over again you will repeat this process, altering the quality of your moments and the capacity of your brain to be more conscious.

Over time, regular micro-doses of mindfulness will increase your brain's attention span and deepen your connection with yourself, others, and the world around you.

You will strengthen your ability to be in the present moment throughout your day, not just for a few moments.

These are the benefits the Mindful Distraction technique will help you achieve.

Mindful Distraction uses distractions in a positive way by seeing them as reminders to practice focus and become mindful for a moment. The very distractions that harm you are now benefiting you by helping you make a habit of paying attention. They become a trigger to create a moment of mindful attention.

With this technique, you disconnect from the digital world for a moment: instead of directing your attention outward, you redirect it inward. By doing so, you redirect your energy back to yourself. Because your attention is energy. While the digital world is trying to pull your attention—and therefore your energy—outward, Mindful Distraction directs your attention and your energy inward. You conserve your energy and let your mind have a moment of rest.

> While the digital world is trying to pull your attention—and therefore your energy—outward, Mindful Distraction directs your attention and your energy inward. You conserve your energy and let your mind have a moment of rest.

Doing the Mindful Distraction technique takes no extra time, but it adds significant benefit to your day. It may even give you more time, as it increases your productivity, creativity, relaxation, and happiness. It recharges you again and again.

Our sense of time is different when we have a sense of hurry or when we are in a state of calmness. You can slow down your sense of rush by introducing micro-doses of mindfulness into your day.

How to Do the *Mindful Distraction* Technique

The Mindful Distraction technique uses distraction in a positive way. We let a distraction be a reminder to practice a moment of mindfulness.

To do this technique:

Step 1: *Notice the distraction.*

Whenever you hear a notification sound from your digital devices, notice that the sound caused your mind to become distracted.

Step 2: *Take a pause.*

Before you reach out to check your device, pause for a moment.

Step 3: *Take one mindful breath.*

In the moment of pause, take one slow, deep breath with full attention. For one moment disconnect from all your activity and the digital world and connect with yourself and be fully present with your breath. For one inhale and one exhale, be with your breath completely, as if the whole world has disappeared and only you and your breath exist. As you inhale, pay attention to the air going into your body and as you exhale pay attention to the air coming out of your body.

You can deepen the moment of mindfulness by feeling the joy of having this breath and this gift of life and appreciating this gift.

And to deepen it even further, you can show appreciation for this gift by bringing a smile to your face.

After this one moment of mindfulness, you can continue your activity or reach for your device.

You don't have to do the Mindful Distraction technique when a device alert distracts you. You can do it when *anything* distracts you, even your own mind. For example, when you feel the compulsion to check your phone without any notification to trigger you, use this moment of distraction to do one Mindful Distraction moment as described.

The *Mindful Distraction* Technique in Action

Mindful Distraction worked well for Tom, who used to get anxious whenever he heard his phone ring. Tom is an operations manager who started to work at a new company about a year before he encountered the Mindful Distraction technique. His new job was not what he had hoped for.

Tom was having a problem with his boss, who would change his plans and instructions at the last minute and create extra work for Tom. What bothered him the most were the after-hours phone calls to discuss an assignment due the next day.

Gradually, Tom became anxious every time his phone rang, worrying it might be his boss with a last-minute deadline or change of plans. This added to the stress that he was already experiencing at work. One day, he saw one of my articles on Mindful Distraction in a magazine and decided to give it a try.

Whenever he heard his phone ring, he would take a deep breath and pay attention to his breath. Only then would he answer the phone. He found that this simple practice allowed him to shift his attention away from his anxiety about the call. Soon he realized he was calmer when he did the Mindful Distraction technique before answering the phone. He started to expand this practice and do it before checking his emails and voice mail messages, too.

Gradually the ring of his phone and other device alerts became triggers for Tom to relax. He was able to overcome his anxiety and, as he became more in control of his stress, his performance at work improved.

Tom also found that he was better able to handle his boss's attitude when he answered the phone with less stress. And sometimes he has been able to find a way to say no to extra work without negatively impacting his work relationship with his boss.

His time at home was more relaxed, too, because he didn't take his stress and the tension of the work home to his wife and kids. Tom was able to enjoy his time at home with his family more.

Many months after starting to use Mindful Distraction, Tom wrote to me to say how this technique had helped him. He attended one of my meditation classes and started adding more simple meditation techniques to his daily routine. Once you taste the flavor of joy and relaxation, you want to keep enjoying it.

Tom still works at the same company, but now he knows how to manage his mind so that he is not shaken by the outside environment.

Mary also found Mindful Distraction extremely helpful. Mary is a busy mom of three kids ages nine, seven, and three. She is also an engineer and works as the head of R&D at a very large company. Being so busy, she never had time to sleep enough or sometimes even eat. She found her brain didn't always cooperate with her. She would forget things regularly, which she found annoying and concerning. She knew she needed to do something to calm her mind, and she knew the benefits of meditation and mindfulness, but she didn't have time to practice them.

One day a friend sent her one of my magazine articles on Mindful Distraction. She liked the idea, even though she didn't use her phone much. She didn't use social media and turned the notification sounds on her phone off except for phone calls and voice mail messages.

Mary decided to use the technique whenever she was interrupted at work by coworkers and when she would get annoyed at her kids for screaming, jumping, fighting, or running around the house.

At these times, she paused for a moment, took a deep breath, and put her whole focus on her breath. She enjoyed those small moments of inner silence and being with herself for a moment despite the outside noise. She found it grounding and calming. She liked the idea of micro-mindfulness, which she thought worked perfectly for her as a busy mom and would for anyone who doesn't have much time to relax.

Now, she says she is always looking for some new reminders to add micro-mindfulness moments to her life, to find more chances to relax for a moment throughout her day.

James also benefited from the Mindful Distraction technique. James is an architect. I first met him when he attended one of my talks about happiness. He liked the idea of the Mindful Distraction technique and decided to practice it. He realized he was addicted to his smartphone and couldn't live without it. His phone would constantly beep with notifications from his social media accounts, messages, emails, and apps. He would immediately reach out to check his phone after each beep.

> Our breath is a powerful tool to release stress and reduce tension in our bodies. How we breathe and how we feel are connected.

He liked the idea of being free from this addiction, especially when he learned that constant distraction could have a negative impact on his productivity, ability to focus, and his happiness level. He suspected his dependence on his phone was causing him anxiety.

He practiced Mindful Distraction technique for six months before he wrote to me to say how much it helped him become more focused. He still had cravings to use his phone, but he felt that his sense of urgency to check it was lowering and he was becoming more productive. By adding a positive aspect—being mindful—to his phone habit, James didn't feel as guilty for being addicted to his phone.

He believes that frequent mindful moments help him feel more relaxed and he wants to have more of them. He has a strong sense of satisfaction for creating a positive change in his life with his conscious effort.

The Significance of the *Mindful Distraction* Technique

In this digital world of distraction, where ads, apps, and notifications demand our notice, the best gift we can give ourselves is to regain our attention. The Mindful Distraction technique is the simplest way to do that.

Taking a slow, deep breath is a highly effective way to calm the mind. Paying attention to your breath is also quite effective at increasing your focus and connecting you with life on a deeper level.

Our breath is a powerful tool to release stress and reduce tension in our bodies.

How we breathe and how we feel are connected. When we are stressed, we tend to breathe shallowly, holding our breath and taking in less air. When we are relaxed, we breathe slowly and deeply.

When you consciously take a slow, deep breath, you send the message to your brain that you are safe and you can relax. It calms your nervous system, lowers your blood pressure, reduces your heart rate, relaxes your muscles, and decreases stress and anxiety.

These small doses of mindfulness rest your mind and relax your body. They pause the constant stream of outside stimuli competing for your attention and bring you back to the richness of the moment and the life in it.

We need to stay in our moments to enjoy them and to connect with them. Our moments do not last forever. Each moment is precious, as it is here for just a brief time and it will never come back.

We are too busy living that we forget to *live*, we forget to pause and to enjoy. Bringing full attention to your present moment is an effective strategy to make better use of each moment and enjoy life fully.

The Mindful Distraction technique helps you stay in the moment by replacing the unconscious habit of distraction with the conscious habit of focus.

Considering adults check their phones fifty times a day, and this number is increasing, you likely have many opportunities throughout your waking hours to use this practice to instill the habit of being mindful and start enjoying the many benefits of mindfulness.

Become mindful for one breath and feel a breeze cool down your overheated busy mind, refreshing your soul for a moment, before returning to the overstimulating world we live in.

In this digital world of distraction and constant connectivity, we need to cultivate the ability to focus in order to distract-proof our mind.

The more you face distraction, the more you need to train your mindful muscles. And with Mindful Distraction, the more you face distraction, the more you have a trigger to remind you to be mindful. It is an effective strategy to increase focus, heal your pains and unlock your best life.

CHAPTER 5

EMBRACE GRATITUDE

WHEN I WENT to the integrative clinic to start my treatments for Lyme disease, the doctors needed me to take a series of comprehensive tests to see what was going on in my body. It was going to be a long day. And I was already feeling exhausted.

First, I had to answer more than two hundred pages of questions. It took me more than ninety minutes to complete. Then the doctors needed to take some measurements of my body.

One particular test they wanted to do that day required my body to be relaxed in order for the results to be reliable and accurate. As the nurse and I moved through the various tests one by one, she checked a monitor to see if my body was relaxed enough to do that particular test. But my fatigued body was not relaxed enough.

Two hours passed. We had almost completed all of the tests and my body still wasn't relaxed enough. I was becoming increasingly tired and impatient after the long hours in the clinic, and I was hoping to go home soon and have a rest. I tried to be more relaxed so my body would relax more, even though I knew that the very *attempt* to relax makes it impossible. One moment I'd become intensely focused, desperately trying to relax, and the next moment I'd remind myself that it's a futile attempt, because the tension itself would take me further away from a state of relaxation. And I would let go of the attempt.

Then my mind would tell me, "You were lying down here for two hours and you thought you were relaxed, but apparently it wasn't enough. You should do something to bring yourself to a deeper relaxation state." And I'd try again. I was moving between these states of tension and release for a few minutes when suddenly something shifted in my mind.

I became aware of my present moment on a deeper level and I could see my situation in that moment with a broader view: I was comfortably lying down. Soft, relaxing music was playing. My wonderful husband was sitting in front of me. And the nurse was doing the measurements with care.

Suddenly I became aware of all this and I thought, "I am so blessed that I am here with my loving husband. And someone whom I don't know and who doesn't know me is helping me by doing these tests with so much care. And there is a good doctor who will check the results of these tests and provide me the best treatments. And I am doing nothing. I'm just lying down here and relaxing and everything is being done for me."

With this thought, I felt deeply grateful that existence has given me so many blessings by providing me with all these supports, and all I needed to do was just lie down and relax.

The moment I felt this gratitude, something changed. Instantly I felt at ease and very relaxed. I felt a sense of love, a subtle warmness pouring into me from all directions. My body felt lighter. And my heart felt full.

A couple of seconds later, the nurse looked at the monitor and said, "Your body is relaxed now. Now we can do that test." I was amazed to hear that. The nurse had not been aware of my thoughts or feelings. It was the electrodes that picked up the signals from my heart and showed the relaxation of my body on the monitor as a response to my feeling of gratitude.

Although I had sensed that something changed in my body when that deep feeling of gratitude came to me, seeing it being physically measured by machines was a powerful testimony to how our thoughts and our feelings can have instantaneous and quantifiable effects on our body.

The Power of Gratitude

Practicing gratitude is one of the most powerful exercises to train your mind and change your brain to stay positive and focus on the positive. Gratitude switches off the survival mode of the brain by turning on the conscious mode. It is one of the most effective ways to create a happy mind and improve your sense of well-being.

Gratitude is about recognizing and appreciating the good things in life. It is a practice to focus more on what you have instead of what you lack. It focuses your attention on the positive and therefore shifts your attention away from the negatives in life.

The fact is that everyone, at each moment, has both positives and negatives available to focus on. An untrained mind that spends more time in survival mode tends to look for the negatives and ignore the positives.

Practicing gratitude expands our ability to have a wider view of life and to see the positives instead of ignoring them. And it takes us one step further than just seeing them; it helps us to appreciate them.

If we don't consciously cultivate a mind that looks for the positives and appreciates them, we will easily get caught up in all the negatives and overlook all the good.

Having a wider view also gives us a more realistic and clearer view of our situation. With a narrow, distorted view we ignore and overlook important elements.

> Practicing gratitude expands our ability to have a wider view of life and to see the positives instead of ignoring them. And it takes us one step further than just seeing them; it helps us to appreciate them.

For example, you may have a pain in your leg or someone might insult you. With a trained mind that is cultivated by gratitude, you will see that this is a small thing among the many things in your day.

You will also see that your heart is beating in your chest, all your organs are functioning well—your liver, pancreas, gallbladder, kidney, lungs, brain, etc.—and you have 50 billion cells that are working in great synchronicity to keep your body and your life functioning. Besides, the sun is up there in the sky providing energy to this planet, trees are releasing oxygen for you to breathe, and your loved ones are with you, showing you affection, love, and care. Many people in different parts of the world are working different kinds of jobs so that you may have food, clothing, electronics, and other benefits of the global interconnection.

Consider the coffee or tea you drink in the morning, the food you eat, the clean water you drink, the clothes you are wearing right now, the electricity you use. Can you imagine one week without electricity? All this and more is available to you because of other people's efforts in every corner of the globe.

If you can recognize and appreciate everything else going on in your body and in the world, your sore leg or bruised feelings don't look so important anymore. You know your life is about more than this one aspect—the pain in your leg or your mind. Taking your attention away from the pain and seeing a wider view of life may even lessen the pain.

Seeing the bigger picture and recognizing and focusing on the positive expands our life beyond survival.

It is easy to become negative in times of difficulty or pain of any sort that causes our minds to perceive a threat to our survival. During such times, we must strive to maintain a positive mind so we can shift our brain to conscious or healing mode.

It is easier to not get caught up in pain when you can truly see the countless blessings available to you in each moment. By noticing these blessings you will see and feel the abundance that fills up every moment of your life. The momentary pain will eventually go away, but the abundance of life will remain with you at every moment. You will find a sense of trust, a sense of peace, in your heart that you are taken care of. And you will feel a sense of belonging to this universal process of life that you are part of.

A simple practice of gratitude and a simple shift in your mind can radically change your perception of life.

Remember, outside circumstances do not shape your experiences. How you *perceive* your circumstances determines your experience. And how you perceive happens in your mind.

Problems are signs that something is moving you away from your true self. Problems can be viewed as opportunities for growth if you examine the problem to find out what it is about your mindset, beliefs, or choices that is moving you away from living the life you truly want and then to fix it.

Gratitude trains your mind to perceive your experiences in a life-affirming, supportive way. Your mind is less likely to flip to survival mode, even in times of pain, challenge, or uncertainty.

Even pain can be viewed as a positive if you view it as a sign to notice that something is causing damage to your body or your life. Without the pain, you wouldn't be aware of the damage and you wouldn't look for a way to fix the cause of it. The damage would continue and perhaps threaten your life.

For example, if a thorn pierces your foot, it is better to feel pain so you become aware of it and can remove the thorn before it causes serious damage.

Problems are signs that something is moving you away from your true self. Problems can be viewed as opportunities for growth if you examine the problem to find out what it is about your mindset, beliefs, or choices that is moving you away from living the life you truly want and then to fix it.

How we label life events as either "positive" or "negative" depends on how we perceive those events, not the events themselves.

We see the world through the lenses of our minds. Therefore, how your mind views the world is critical to how you perceive the world. You are not separate from your life experiences. As quantum mechanics shows us, the observer and the observed together make the experience of observation. Your mind is the instrument that observes and gives meaning to what is being observed. It is important to have a more realistic view of the world rather than a distorted view.

The Mind Compares

And our mind works by comparing.

We receive information from the outside world through our five senses and our minds interpret the data and give it meaning. To interpret the data, our minds compare it to data already stored in their archives, our past experiences and acquired knowledge.

How we perceive reality is based on comparison.

Most of what we perceive as reality is *perceived* reality. Relative, not absolute. For example, sitting still in your room, you perceive that you are not moving. You are not *really* still; you are still only in comparison to Earth. An astronaut looking at you from space would see that you are moving, as the Earth is moving. And the astronaut is moving as well.

> Everything in your mind is perceived in comparison with something else. Based on the comparison, you add labels such as good or bad, right or wrong, positive or negative, big or small to people, objects, and events.

In fact, nothing is still in this physical world. Everything, from galaxies to electrons, is moving. There is no stillness as such in the physical world. However, we sometimes perceive ourselves or others as still in comparison to other objects.

Similarly, everything in your mind is perceived in comparison with something else. Based on the comparison, you add labels such as good or bad, right or wrong, positive or negative, big or small to people, objects, and events.

Look at the line below (figure 5.1). Is it big or small?

Figure 5.1

The answer is: It depends. It is neither big nor small on its own. It becomes big or small when you compare it with another line. Look at this line compared to line 1 in figure 5.2. Then, it becomes small. Now compare it with line 2 and it becomes big.

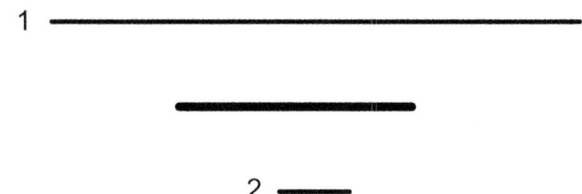

Figure 5.2 The line in the middle is "small" when compared to line 1 and "big" when compared to line 2.

I call this exercise *the line comparison model,* and it clearly illustrates that the line in the middle has no objective size, only the size your mind perceives it to have based on a comparison to another line.

Or say Steve has $1,000 in his bank account and feels rich because he compares it with the fact that he has never had $1,000 before. Or he compares his wealth to that of his neighbors, who do not have as much money. Sheryl has $100,000 in her bank account and feels poor because she compares it to when she had over a million dollars in her bank account. Or she compares it to her friend's account, which is much higher.

How we perceive and feel about our life situations depends on what we compare them with in our minds.

Expectation Can Make Us Unhappy

When we view our life situations, we usually compare them with our expectations of how they should be. An untrained mind doesn't see things as they are. Like the example above, the line is just a line, it is not a big or a small line, until we start comparing it with something else. Then it gets the label of big or small.

Events in our lives are also just events. They are not positive or negative—until we start comparing them to a frame of reference in our minds. And depending on our expectations, the labels we give to our life events can make us happy or unhappy.

After a conference, my colleagues at my workplace at the university in Sydney organized for the speakers an expensive dinner party at a fancy restaurant famous for its cuisine. The organizers had not been to this restaurant before but they had heard a lot about it and chose it, even though it was over their budget. They wanted to show their special guests the highest standard of hospitality.

In the days leading up to the dinner, I heard my colleagues talking about this restaurant over and over. They were excited and looked forward to visiting. The day arrived and we went to the

> Whether we are grateful or not does not depend on what we have; it depends on how we perceive what we have. And this perception depends on the lenses in our minds with which we look at life.

restaurant. The dishes came one by one. They were all good, and I enjoyed them. But they didn't meet the high expectations we all had after hearing so many rave reviews. The day after the party, I heard all my colleagues say that the dishes were not as good as they'd expected. The organizers were very disappointed.

If the organizers had not had such high expectation about that restaurant, they wouldn't have been disappointed. The meal was good on its own, but it wasn't as special as they had anticipated.

Our expectations affect our experiences.

Whether we are grateful or not does not depend on what we have; it depends on how we perceive what we have. And this perception depends on the lenses in our minds with which we look at life.

Our minds can make us not enjoy our lives in spite of all the blessings that we have or it can help us enjoy our lives no matter what. It depends on how it perceives our circumstances. An untrained mind that works in survival mode tends to lean toward the negative side of things, ignoring the positive side, taking it for granted, or simply getting so used to the positive that it no longer appreciates it.

Train Your Mind, Claim Your Life

Because the untrained mind leans toward negativity, it is important to train our minds. And that's why we need to meddle and consciously choose what we want to focus on instead of letting our minds work by default.

We can train our minds to have a more realistic view of life, to see more than only what it perceives as negative and stop ignoring all the positives. We can expand our mindset and consciously suggest new points of reference to improve our perception of our life situations.

We can wonder at the blessings contained in each moment instead of comparing it to our expectations of how it should be. We can consciously look for the positive and appreciate it instead of overlooking it.

> We can wonder at the blessings contained in each moment instead of comparing it to our expectations of how it should be. We can consciously look for the positive and appreciate it instead of overlooking it.

Training our mind in this way encourages it to look for abundance instead of lack, blessings instead of curses, opportunities instead of problems.

A given situation can be perceived as either positive or negative. The label you give it depends on which side you want to see.

Take the earlier examples of Steve and Sheryl. One person can have $1,000 and be happy about it while another can have $100,000 and be unhappy. Their happiness does not depend on how much money they have. It depends on how they perceive what they have, what they compare it to, and what they focus on.

By seeing the positive and appreciating it, we shift our minds to experience our lives in a more positive way. Life is growth. If, for example, we see every event as an opportunity, then we look for how we can grow even from pain and challenges. We let difficulties enhance our experience of life instead of degrading it.

Jack and Joe both lost their jobs during the recession. Jack looks at it this way: I lost my source of income. In this recession, it is so difficult to find a job. What am I going to do? How am I going to pay the rent? Why did they fire me and not the other person? I was working hard for them and they didn't know the value of my work. I'm so disappointed. Was this the answer to all my hard work for this company?

The situation is difficult for Jack. These thoughts may be true or some of them may be an exaggeration. However, in this difficult situation, getting lost in these negative thoughts and going on a downward spiral is not helping Jack solve his problem or find a new job.

Here is where seeing a broader view of his life situation and shifting to the conscious mode with a technique like gratitude can help Jack have a better outcome in this challenging time. By shifting his mind from his survival-based reaction, Jack could use his mental resources and his energy to look for a new job or another source of income, maybe even find a better employment situation than his previous one. With the shift, Jack has the potential for a positive outcome.

Let's look at how Joe responds to a similar situation.

Joe looks at it this way: I'm disappointed that they fired me. But what can I do? It's the recession and many people have lost their jobs, and now I'm one of them. I wasn't enjoying that job anyway. I was always thinking of opening my own business, but this job was keeping me busy, and I always wished I had more time. Well, I guess now I have the time I was wishing for. I have my savings and I can use that to cover my expenses for a few months. I can take a few days of vacation to relax. And then I should make a plan to start learning the skills that I need to finally start my own business. This is an opportunity for me to start working on what I've wanted to do. I'm grateful for this opportunity.

By cultivating a grateful mind, we train our minds to look for opportunities even in problems. And we consciously create better outcomes and better experiences.

The Benefits of the *Embrace Gratitude* Technique

Gratitude, a simple shift in our mindset to focus on the blessings hidden in every moment, brings many benefits.

Research in positive psychology shows that gratitude is strongly associated with a wide range of physical, psychological, and social benefits, including increased happiness,[21] greater life satisfaction and self-esteem,[22] a stronger immune system,[23] more optimism, better sleep,[24] more energy,[25] reduced depression, reduced physical pain[26] and more.

According to Dr. Robert Emmons, professor of psychology at the University of California and one of the world's leading scientific experts on gratitude, "The growing

> By cultivating a grateful mind, we train our minds to look for opportunities even in problems. And we consciously create better outcomes and better experiences.

evidence suggests that gratitude is a key element for sparking positive and sustained changes in individual well-being."[27]

When we practice gratitude and focus on positive thoughts, we activate the conscious mode of our brain and switch off survival mode. Shifting to positive thoughts triggers the production of feel-good chemicals, such as dopamine and serotonin, that create a sense of happiness within us. We develop a happy mind. And a happy mind is a healing mind, able to heal our pain and unlock our best life.

Gratitude expands our minds to understand that we have a choice about which thought to focus on. The pain or the blessing? Which one we choose makes all the difference in how we experience life. Gratitude helps us to consciously choose to focus on the blessings rather than the pain or problem.

> Gratitude makes your life richer. It grows your mind to look for and recognize the blessings hidden in every moment of life. With such a mind, you will see abundance instead of lack in every moment of life. Then the rush to get into the next moment with the hope to find satisfaction there (rather than staying here) will recede.

Shifting our attention away from our pain and problems and putting our attention on our blessings waters the potted plant associated with positive thoughts, helping it grow while letting the potted plant of negative thoughts wither.

And the amazing fact is that the pain then takes care of itself. Spending your energy and attention watering positive thoughts and feelings produces healing chemicals in your body. Whether your pain is physical, emotional, or mental, it will lessen or you will be less bothered by it.

Besides, gratitude makes your life richer. As Eckhart Tolle says in his book *The Power of Now*, "Gratitude for the present moment and the fullness of life *now* is true prosperity."[28] It grows your mind to look for and recognize the blessings hidden in every moment of life. With such a mind, you will see abundance instead of lack in every moment of life. Then the rush to get into the next moment with the hope to find satisfaction there (rather than staying here) will recede. You will relax in the present moment and you will find satisfaction and happiness in it.

Abundance is always here in the present moment. Cultivating gratitude enhances your ability to detect it. Imagine your mind as a radio that can tune into many different channels on a variety of frequencies. There are many radio channels available at different frequencies right here, right now. Until you tune into the frequency of gratitude, you won't be able to hear the music on the channel of abundance.

The beauty of practicing gratitude is that the dopamine produced in your brain when you feel grateful is involved in the brain's reward system. It creates what neuroscientist Dr. Alex Korb calls a "virtuous cycle," which means the more you practice gratitude the easier it gets for your brain to look for things to be grateful about. Your brain gets wired for more positivity and more gratitude.

How to Do the *Embrace Gratitude* Technique

This is a simple practice to bring gratitude to your daily routine. At least once a day, pause to reflect on the present moment and the blessings you have. Identify at least three blessings. For each blessing, follow the steps below.

Step 1: *See the blessing.*

Think about how this blessing enriches your life.

Visualize this blessing and imagine what this blessing makes possible for you to experience.

Step 2: *Feel the blessing.*

Feel gratitude for all the positive feelings this blessing gives you.

You must *genuinely* feel grateful and appreciative to trigger the feel-good chemicals in your body and reap their benefits.

Step 3: *Imagine your life without this blessing. (Optional)*

Just for one moment, imagine what your life would be like if you didn't have this blessing.

Since the objective of this practice is to focus on the blessing, not the lack of it, don't spend more than a second on this step. Just think for a moment what life would be like without this blessing, so that you realize its value even more. This can help you feel appreciative for your blessing on a deeper level.

Step 4: *Give thanks for the blessing.*

Say thank you for having this blessing in your life.

Do this technique at least once a day every day to bring yourself to a state of gratitude. In addition, do this practice every time you feel mental, emotional, or physical pain or face a stressful event.

The *Embrace Gratitude* Technique in Action

Practicing gratitude changed Helen's relationship with pain. Helen was one of my first meditation students. A schoolteacher in her late fifties, she had an accident in her twenties that injured her back. She had a couple of surgeries but she never fully recovered and was living with chronic pain in her back and her legs.

She liked the gratitude practice that she learned in my meditation class. She found that practicing gratitude shifted her mind away from the pain and helped her focus on the good things that she has in her life. She says that sometimes she momentarily forgets the pain when she is focused on her blessings and feeling grateful for them. In fact, her pain became a reason for her to practice gratitude often during the day. And she feels that she is becoming happier because of her frequent practice.

Before her gratitude practice, she was very frustrated by the pain, and she would focus on it and how much she doesn't want it. But now she sees that focusing on her blessings helps her relax, and this soothes her pain.

Ashley found focusing on her blessings an effective way to help her stay positive during the coronavirus pandemic lockdown in 2020. Ashley attended one of my programs on how to reduce stress at the company where she was working. One of her favorite tools was the gratitude practice that she learned in the program. And she started to practice it.

When the COVID-19 pandemic started, she could see the importance of holding on to this important practice and believes gratitude helped her stay in control of her mind, manage her stress, and stay peaceful and positive during the pandemic.

Fear, anxiety, and uncertainty surrounded her, but she knew she could choose which thoughts and feelings to focus her mind on. So, every day she would focus on her blessings, appreciate them, and feel grateful for them.

> Happiness is a state of mind that can be cultivated from the inside. When you know how to manage your mind and have the wisdom to focus on positive thoughts, you can be happy right now regardless of your circumstances.

She would focus on the fact that she has a home, a job that allows her to work from home, and a healthy family. And she felt grateful for her company that provided her with the opportunity to learn a technique to help her manage her stress.

Focusing on the positive things that she had in her life would shift her mind away from the survival mode and the worry and fear would recede.

She believes the lockdown and all of the confusion and panic in the world made her more aware of many of the blessings she had been taking for granted, such as the ability to easily find everything she wants in a store, to leave home without worry over catching a virus that could threaten her and her family's lives, to hug her friends, and to go to the beach.

Helen and Ashley reduced their mental and physical pain through a simple practice of gratitude. A slight mind shift can greatly improve our lives.

The Significance of the *Embrace Gratitude* Technique

Cultivating gratitude is one of the most effective ways to create a positive, happy, and healing mind. It is the wisest way to heal your pain and enrich your life.

A grateful mind brings us to a state of ease, a state of happiness that springs from within. It is not dependent on the external world.

Happiness is a state of mind that can be cultivated from the inside. We don't have to wait for the externals of life to be perfectly aligned with what we expect them to be in order to be happy. When you know how to manage your mind and have the wisdom to focus on positive thoughts, you can be happy right now regardless of your circumstances.

> With a happy mind, you have less fear, stress, anxiety, and other negative emotions that prevent you from functioning at your best. With a happy mind, you are more productive, energetic, and enthusiastic about life and all it has to offer.

This does not mean that you should become passive and not work to create the external successes that you want. The opposite. With gratitude, you are better able to create the outcomes you desire. With a happy mind, you have less fear, stress, anxiety, and other negative emotions that prevent you from functioning at your best. With a happy mind, you are more productive, energetic, and enthusiastic about life and all it has to offer. You become more focused and creative and a better decision maker. You can use your capabilities to their fullest potential to create the life that you want.

Yet your happiness doesn't depend on your achievements because you are *already* happy. Achievements, whether wealth, power, social capital, or knowledge, are accessories, and as Sadhguru, the Indian yogi and mystic, teaches, life itself is a far more significant phenomenon than any of the accessories we decorate it with.

With gratitude, we realize that life is our most valuable blessing. Life is so immense and so magnificent (and so mysterious) that every problem pales in importance. Being bothered by what we perceive as problems is based on fear. And paraphrasing Osho, all our fears are basically fear of losing this life.

We know the value of this life. However, when we live in a rush, we miss the magnificence of what is happening in the present moment. We miss the good things that support and sustain our lives such as the sun, stars, and trees, and we mostly see and often imagine only what threatens us. When we live in a rush, we live in survival mode.

Being grateful switches your brain to conscious mode and unlocks your potential to create the future you want.

CHAPTER 6

DESCRIBE THE MOMENT

ONE EVENING, I was taking a walk in the park near my apartment in Sydney with my husband, Farshid. We were strolling next to a beautiful lake, one of many that dotted the area. The sky was covered with thick clouds and it had just started to rain. I wasn't feeling well. It was a few months into my treatments for Lyme disease, and my body was extremely fatigued and my mind agitated. I knew spending some time in nature and moving my body would do me some good.

As we were walking, I started to talk about a random subject that came to my mind. I quickly noticed that Farshid was not listening. He was lost in his thoughts. I knew he had had a busy day at work, but I noticed that I was getting annoyed that he was not listening. Normally, this wouldn't offend me but today his behavior was irritating my hyper mind, already struggling to deal with the toxins circulating in my body.

I knew that if I didn't take control of my mind immediately, I would grow increasingly agitated and upset for no good reason and exacerbate discomfort in my body. Farshid would notice and grow upset as well. I knew that I needed to make myself conscious of the present moment and switch off my survival-based reaction.

So, I immediately started describing the moment to myself to help me keep my focus on it. This was one of the strategies I relied on to keep my mind focused on what empowers me.

As I noticed the world around me, time slowed down. My senses became more receptive to capture the wonders of that moment.

And it was a magical moment. The thick clouds in the sky looked mysteriously beautiful. Drops of rain were creating a beautiful pattern of thousands of small ripples on the water. The gentle sound of the drops of rain landing on my umbrella one by one was like a relaxing music to my ears. Two birds were flying in the sky passing over us from far above. The air was so fresh. The trees looked refreshed from the rain and the leaves were dancing in the gentle wind.

Everything seemed to be celebrating that moment.

In my mind, I transformed all of these elements into three short phrases, a short poem. Later, I wrote the poem in my journal:

> Sound of rain drops on my umbrella
> Flying birds
> Disappear in the clouds

Focusing on the present moment helped me stay in control of my mind and bring it into conscious mode. I came back to my senses to see the beauty around me and I felt grateful for this exquisite moment. I was surrounded with miracles and wonder. It was utterly peaceful and at ease.

This peace and ease had always been there, but it flew into me when I paid attention to it and connected with it. Keeping my focus on the present moment helped me to tune in.

A smile was inevitable.

I had started this practice of describing the moment more than a year earlier. It was inspired by *haiku*, a condensed form of Japanese poetry dating back hundreds of years ago.

Originally, haiku was the opening part of a complex tradition of Japanese poetry, called *renga*. In the seventeenth century, Matsuo Bashō, one of the greatest Japanese poets, perfected the form as an independent poem. It was called *hokku* then. Not until the late nineteenth century was it renamed "haiku" by the Japanese poet Masaoka Shiki.

Haiku

A haiku is composed of three short phrases describing one's experience objectively. Traditionally, haiku captures a moment of connection with nature that expresses an understanding or realization about the nature of life, an aha moment.

The significance of haiku is that it presents an *objective* presentation of the experience. The poet paints a scene with words using simple, nondescriptive language without mentioning what they feel about the scene. The intention is to allow the reader to see the image and feel the revelation for themselves.

To do so, a haiku conveys what the poet receives in the present moment from the five senses. It captures the immediate experience in the present moment without further explanation or judgment.

This is one of the most famous haiku from Matsuo Bashō:

> The old pond
> A frog jumps in—
> Plop!
>
> —Translated by R. H. Blyth

This appears to be a description of a simple, ordinary event. But it is profound because it shows that the ordinary can become extraordinary. This poem contains the meaning of creation itself.

With few words, this haiku transfers an image to you and invites you to have an experience. It takes you to that moment to feel the silence of the old pond, to see the movement of the frog jumping into the water, to hear the sound of the water, to notice the old pond returning to silence again.

But it doesn't describe any of it to you. It invites you to participate in creating the old pond, the frog, the ripples, all of it, just the way you want it.

And once you look deeper into this ordinary scene, the sudden break of the silence of the old pond by the jump of the frog might ignite an insight in you, an aha moment. To me it can be an anecdote for existence from the beginning to the end: silence, movement, sound (big bang), ripples (vibrations), silence again.

The wisdom of haiku, simplifying things to transfer their profundity, inspired me to pay attention to the depth of simplicity in the moments in my life. And I started a practice that I call the *Describe the Moment*[29] technique to help me see the moments more attentively.

I found that describing what my five senses receive in the present moment without interpretation helps me remain in the moment with more focus and brings me closer to the reality contained in that moment.

Be Present, Be Pleasant

It is important to remain in the present moment and to see the present moment as it is. Because life is happening in the present moment. Every process, every movement, every event takes place in the now. Only when we are in the present moment can we connect with life and what is happening in it.

The problem is that our lives are happening in the now, but we are living in our minds, which live everywhere but in the now. We live in the past or the future most of the time, missing the now, the only reality available to us.

If we are not conscious of our moments, our mind gets distracted and it starts wandering, taking us to the memories of the past or imaginations about the future. Memory is a replay of a scene that was once real, but not anymore. And imagination is an assumption that may become real one day or may not. Both memory and imagination are like movies on a screen. They are not real.

However, our distracted minds are not trained to pay attention to what is happening in the now. If we are not connected with the present moment, we miss connecting with the simple things that enrich our lives: the laughter of a child, the hug of a loved one, the cool breeze of the morning touching our face. And we miss the fact that each moment that passes by is a moment that never comes back.

When we focus on the now, we become receptive to life, to see its beauties and the blessings disguised in the ordinary moments.

To appreciate life, we need to develop our ability to focus and remain in the now.

You might think it sounds easy to remain in the moment but when you start practicing you will notice how easily your mind gets distracted and starts wandering to the past or the future. This is our survival brain asserting its control to protect us from danger.

> It is important to remain in the present moment and to see the present moment as it is. Because life is happening in the present moment. Every process, every movement, every event takes place in the now. Only when we are in the present moment can we connect with life and what is happening in it.

Survival mode is more active when your day is busy, you have a feeling of hurriedness, or you're stressed, anxious, depressed, or in physical pain. During those times, your mind tends to get distracted more easily and it is more difficult to remain in the moment. However, staying in the moment calms the mind and heals the pain.

That's why it is especially important to be able to remain conscious and anchored in the now in such moments, even though it is more difficult.

By paying attention to what is happening in the present moment, you shift your attention away from what is not real, the thoughts, memories, or imaginations in your mind, and bring yourself back to what is real, the present moment.

It also switches on our conscious mode while switching off survival mode.

One way to keep your attention focused on what is real in the now is the Describe the Moment technique.

The Benefits of the *Describe the Moment* Technique

In my experiments with different practices to train my mind to remain focused in the present moment, I found the Describe the Moment technique an effective tool to help me hold my attention in the moment, even when my mind is agitated.

I noticed that when I want to *describe* my moments, I need to be in the moment more attentively and pay more attention, and that helps me experience the moments with more focus, fully, instead of passing through them superficially.

Moreover, I found that I can see the reality of the moments better when I try to describe directly what I see without adding my interpretation. Interpretations are like colored glasses. They hinder us from seeing things clearly, as they truly are.

Removing the colored glasses of interpretation helps us see life and our moments more clearly.

It is the mind's natural inclination to give meaning to the data it receives from our five senses. If you watch your mind carefully, you might notice that you add a label of liking or disliking to almost everything you encounter. This habit of judgment of the mind is based on a survival mechanism to categorize things as good (safe) or bad (dangerous).

If we want to thrive, we must avoid survival mode as much as possible. Our day-to-day lives are pretty much safe. Instead, we need to enhance our ability to pay attention and to spend more time in conscious mode.

One way to do that is to train the mind to give its full attention to the moment and see things as they are. By doing so, we value each moment instead of ignoring it and ignoring what is happening in it.

Each moment is unique. No moment will repeat itself. The universe is so adventurous, it never creates any moment twice. The shape of clouds crossing the sky is unique at every moment. This shape will never repeat itself. The position of our planet and all the planets and stars in the universe is unique at each moment, as the whole universe is ever evolving and expanding. It will not come back to this exact configuration again. The way you experience your body, your emotions, and your surroundings is unique to this moment. You will never again be exactly as you are right now.

> Each moment is unique. No moment will repeat itself. To fully experience each moment and live life fully, you can train your mind to pay attention to the present moment and to see the uniqueness of each moment.

The universe is in constant progress, always moving forward. It never goes back, as time is only progressive. Each moment is a unique moment which will never come back. There will never be another moment like this one.

And this moment is the only moment that you have. The rest—past and future—are imaginations in your mind, not reality in your life.

To fully experience each moment and live life fully, you can train your mind to pay attention to the present moment and to see the uniqueness of each moment. It requires training but it is a skill anyone can learn.

The Describe the Moment technique will help you practice anchoring yourself in the present moment by paying attention to what your senses receive from the outside world in each moment and noticing it without interpretation or judgment. You'll practice letting your mind be a mirror to reflect the moment as it is without adding a label to it. You'll practice seeing things simply as they are. And you become aware of the automatic judgments of the mind and train your mind to see with more clarity and fewer critiques.

This technique moves you out of survival mode and into conscious mode, the zone of growth and healing.

Another benefit of this practice is that you will connect with your creative side. Creativity is one of the most complex processes of the human brain. When you connect with your creative side, you activate multiple areas of your brain. This stimulates communication between different areas of the brain and boosts its working capacity. The brain has the capacity to modify its connections in response to stimuli—a concept called neuroplasticity, or brain plasticity. And creativity enhances the plasticity of the brain.

Activation of the parts of the brain involved in creativity also switches off the survival part of the brain, reducing stress and helping you feel calm.

You will also learn to look more attentively. You will pay more attention to the moment, to your senses, and to what life is offering you that very second. You may notice the breeze in your hair, the smile of a stranger when you stop at a red light, the singing of the birds in the far distance.

These are simple things. But they are all a part of life. And paying close attention to them, noticing every detail, connects you with life on a deeper level. You train your attention to notice life and all that is in it instead of passing by it hastily.

How to Do the *Describe the Moment* Technique

The Describe the Moment technique is inspired by haiku poetry, but it does not involve writing haiku. In spite of its apparent simplicity, haiku is a complex form of poetry and a deep practice. It has some structural rules as well.

A haiku is composed of 17 sound units in Japanese with an arrangement of 5-7-5. The sound unit is often referred to as syllables in English, although the English syllables do not work the same as Japanese sound units. A haiku of 5-7-5 syllables is written in one line in Japanese, but it is split into three lines in English.

A haiku also has a seasonal element to connect the poem with nature and the passage of time.

And it consists of two different images put together with a pause in between. The pause changes the focus from one image to the other. The contrast or comparison between the two images creates a surprise, an understanding, an aha.

A good example is Bashō's haiku:

The old pond
A frog jumps in—
Plop!

The stillness of the old pond is the first image. The movement of the frog and the sound it creates is the second one.

Writing haiku can be a great practice to connect you with life and the moments in life but it takes a lifetime to master. The Describe the Moment technique incorporates some of the principles of haiku to help you keep your focus on the moment and deepen your connection to it, but it does not require you to follow all of the rules for writing haiku.

Instead, you'll simply describe your direct observation of the moment, without judgment or interpretation, in three phrases. Your intention is to capture an image of the moment, emphasizing the elements in it that inspire you and attract your attention.

Use the following steps to do this technique:

Step 1: *Pay attention to your senses.*

Bring your attention to the present moment and notice what you are receiving from your five senses. What do you see, hear, smell, or taste? What is touching your skin?

Step 2: *Choose your most significant sensations at this moment.*

Choose one or two of the most vivid and inspiring sights, sounds, smells, tastes, or sensations.

Step 3 *Describe the moment.*

Describe those sensations in three short phrases, as if you are creating a snapshot of that moment to share with someone. You don't have to use a sentence. You can use one word or a few words or a phrase.

Mention your direct experience. Try to avoid adjectives, similes, or metaphors. The aim here is not to express what you feel about your experience, but to convey what caused that feeling. This helps you witness the moment directly without entering the dividing quality of the mind that tends to parse experiences into likes and dislikes. It helps you see the moment objectively.

A mind that tends to say "I like it" in one moment will say "I don't like it" in another moment. In this practice, we want to transcend this like-dislike division of the mind and see things as they are.

When you start this practice, you might find that you tend to use adjectives or similes to describe your experience. Allow yourself to do that. It is more important to become aware of your mind's tendencies and gently redirect it to look beyond the labels it imposes. This awareness and the intention of wanting to see things more directly gradually trains your mind to do so. This technique is more about developing relaxed attention, noticing, than establishing rules you must follow.

When I first started this practice, I noticed that I tend to add an adjective to the things that I observe. For example, "beautiful sky," "pretty flower," and "relaxing music." With practice, I use adjectives less but I still notice my mind's tendency to apply them. I allow it and I am conscious of it but I don't try too hard to remove the adjectives. Awareness is the goal, not perfectly performing the technique. The technique is just a tool to make you more aware of the moment and provide your mind with ways to focus on it.

Step 4: *Write it down.*

Write your three short phrases on three lines in a journal or on your phone. Date the poem to keep a record of what you felt at that moment.

Examples of My *Describe the Moment* Poems

Here are examples of three of my Describe the Moment poems.

Empty room
Sound of the flute
Lines of the book mixes with the bird's song

Dry forest
Cry of a bird
Flies away

Wet grass
Shining lake
A bird starts to sing

The *Describe the Moment* Technique in Action

Ethan found the Describe the Moment technique an effective way to reset his mind after a long day of work. He attended my G.R.O.W. program because he wanted to grow his peace of mind and enjoy his life more. He works in a bank and complained that the stress of his work was unnecessarily going home with him. Noticing his interest in my experience living in Japan, I told him about the Describe the Moment technique in one of our sessions, and he gave it a try.

He liked the idea of slowing down by paying close attention to his senses. After practicing this technique a few times, he found he loves it. It's a good way to relax his mind at the end of busy workday. He uses the technique while walking through the parking lot on the way to his car.

Paying attention to his surroundings as he walks helps him wash away the stress of the day. Now, he notices the trees along the road. They remind him of the fruit trees in the backyard of his grandmother's house where he used to spend part of the summer when he was a child.

This practice and the shift in his attention that it causes resets his mind so it is able to notice other dimensions of life besides his work: the trees, sky, and clouds he sees along the way. He arrives home refreshed and peaceful.

This practice has also taught him to pay more attention to his senses during the day when he feels he is getting stressed.

He kindly agreed to share one of his haiku in this book.

Tall trees and blue sky
Me walking slowly
Enjoying the breeze in spring

The Significance of the *Describe the Moment* Technique

Use the Describe the Moment technique when you find your mind is wandering, taking you out of the real world and into your head, or when you find yourself overtaken by negative thoughts and emotions, such as stress, worry, anxiety, sadness, or annoyance.

In such moments, bring yourself back to the present moment by describing the moment. Take yourself back to what is real, what is happening right now, by paying attention to your senses. The automatic thoughts of the mind are not real and they hinder you from seeing the real in the moment. When you pay attention to your senses to see what you're receiving in the moment you shift your focus to what is real in the now.

Then you train your mind to see things as they are without adding labels to them. By removing the labels you take yourself out of the survival mode that is based on dividing things as "good" or "bad."

That's why the Describe the Moment technique encourages you to avoid using adjectives to describe your experience or at least become aware of when you use them. "Beautiful" is a label. It is a pleasing label, but it is still a label. Resetting your mind to avoid labels brings you back into conscious mode, the mode where all healing happens.

The Describe the Moment technique is a simple but highly effective way to train your mind to be in the moment, see it clearly, and appreciate it fully. It's one way to heal your pain and unlock your best life.

> When you pay attention to your senses to see what you're receiving in the moment you shift your focus to what is real in the now. Then you train your mind to see things as they are without adding labels to them.

CHAPTER 7

MAKE CONSCIOUS CHOICES

ONE SPRING MORNING I was sitting in my apartment, reading a good book. It was a beautiful sunny day. I had opened the door to the balcony and I could hear the sound of the leaves from the tree outside rustling in the breeze. Occasional notes of birdsong were music to my ears.

I was enjoying my day immensely. But then suddenly I heard a loud sound, the sound of some type of machine. I felt annoyed because it interrupted the peaceful moment I was in. I went to the balcony to see what was causing the sound and there it was: a leaf blower. A man was blowing leaves off of the cement pathway in front of his apartment and onto the soil where some ferns and flowers were planted.

I looked closely and noticed he was cranking the leaf blower to remove one stubborn leaf from the path. One leaf! The smell of gasoline hit my nostrils. Now I was even more annoyed. I thought,

> We will feel more freedom in our lives if we practice making conscious choices. What life brings our way is not in our hands, but how we respond to it always is.

this person is not only making a lot of noise with this device but he is also polluting the environment to move just one leaf! Can't he simply bend down and pick it up?

But then I remembered that just as this person can choose how to move the leaf, I can choose to be annoyed or not to be annoyed.

I chose to be peaceful and happy. I started to be mindful of the moment. Instead of focusing on the sound of the leaf blower, I listened attentively for other, more pleasant sounds. I realized I could still hear the leaves in the tree and a bird singing.

I continued this practice for a couple of minutes until the sound of the leaf blower stopped. Immediately, the day was again so peaceful and beautiful. I continued paying attention to the sounds of the leaves, birds, and other pleasant noises. Without the roar of the blower, they sounded heavenly. The absence of the loud noise helped me appreciate the peace and beauty around me even more than before. And I felt grateful for that beautiful moment.

We Always Have a Choice

In any moment we have choices available to us. In fact, we make choices at every moment, whether consciously or unconsciously. And these choices affect every aspect of our lives and how we feel about our lives. It is up to you. You choose whether or not a minor noise or major problem bothers you.

Having choices comes with power and responsibility. We will feel more freedom in our lives if we practice making conscious choices. What life brings our way is not in our hands, but how we respond to it always is.

If we leave it up to the survival mode of our brains to react to our life situations automatically, we're not using our ability to make conscious choices. In survival mode our brain reacts based on its survival instinct. It sees danger and leans into the negative side of things. It operates by default.

If I live by default, then when I hear a noise that annoys me while I want to enjoy a peaceful morning, I will feel stressed because something is not going my way and my brain will perceive it as potential danger. But if I become conscious and intervene in this automatic reaction of my brain, then I will notice that I can choose to be peaceful. I can assure myself that there is no danger; it is just a temporary situation.

> Our lives and our life experiences are the result of the choices that we make in every moment.

When I am in conscious mode, I can do what is needed to reduce the annoying noise. I can close the door to reduce it. Or I can focus on the charming sounds that I like to hear. Or I can speak to the person and request him to stop making the noise. Or many other options.

In conscious mode, I can see many different options to choose from to respond to the situation. In survival mode, I'm not aware of my options and my choices. I react by default.

Some of my options in conscious mode are wiser than others, and it is up to me to decide which one I want to choose. And the choice to stay in survival mode or switch to conscious mode is always available.

Know that you have a choice in any given situation and by making conscious choices you can elevate your life experiences and even turn pains and problems into springboards for growth.

We Can Choose a Different Story

Our lives and our life experiences are the result of the choices that we make in every moment. Most of the time, we make choices unconsciously. But those unconscious choices affect our lives just as much as the conscious ones. To elevate our life experiences we should practice being more conscious and making conscious choices.

Instead of staying in survival mode and living on autopilot, you can choose to become more conscious and live deliberately.

On autopilot, our thoughts tend to be negative, as the survival brain looks for what went wrong in the past, or what might go wrong in the future. Our survival brains ignore our positive experiences and remember, even exaggerate, the negative ones. They can give us the false feeling that we are not safe. We think about a negative experience that happened twenty years ago and it makes us re-feel

> When you decide to make a choice about which thoughts you want to think, memories you want to revisit, and dreams of your future you want to have, and you choose the positive ones, you gradually pave a new pathway for the positives.

the negative feeling and re-create in the present the harmful chemicals associated with that in our body.

But we have a choice here.

We can choose to let our minds continue revisiting those hurtful memories and suffer the harm they create. Or we can choose not to think about them any longer and look at our lives from a new angle.

At first, your mind might still bring those negative memories to revisit you every day. There is a paved path for them to come and knock on the door of your mind. That's the law of nature. Energy flows wherever there is the least resistance. When you walk on a path in a jungle a thousand times, you create a paved path. Similarly, over time, your negative memories have created a paved path in your mind. Worries about the future create the same kind of path.

> You can consciously meddle in the story of your life and consciously bring a new view, a new positive thought that helps you expand your mind and makes you feel good.

But when you decide to make a choice about which thoughts you want to think, memories you want to revisit, and dreams of your future you want to have, and you choose the positive ones, you gradually pave a new pathway for the positives.

When you face negatives of any sort, about your past, present, or future, you can challenge those negative thoughts and choose to adopt a different story. You can consciously meddle in the story of your life and consciously bring a new view, a new positive thought that helps you expand your mind and makes you feel good.

Sarah Makes a Choice

What we think in our minds can change how we feel about ourselves, others, and life. Take Sarah.

Sarah is forty-one. She is a medical doctor. She is married to the love of her life, Alan, who is a lawyer. They married twelve years ago and have two beautiful daughters who are seven and five. She loves Alan, but there are things that he did in the past that hurt her feelings. She is carrying the weight of all the small and big things that Alan did that hurt her and made her feel he didn't care about her.

One Sunday afternoon, Sarah is sitting on a chair in their yard, holding a book and watching her two daughters play in the yard with their father. They're running, screaming, and laughing. She notices her daughters are happy and her husband looks happy, but she does not feel happy. She starts to remember some of the things that Alan did or did not do that made her feel unworthy or not enough to be truly loved.

As she remembers all those things, her heart beats fast, her breathing becomes shallow, and her eyes become wet with tears. She realizes she has been feeling depressed for a long time and she does not have a feeling of joy for life.

Sarah's train of thought could proceed in two different ways.

Scenario 1:

> She thinks: Why me? I have done everything I could for him. I have never done anything that would hurt him, but he didn't care about hurting me. When I first met Alan . . . he was different, so enthusiastic and funny.

When I was with him, I felt happy and secure and cherished and adventurous. We were so happy together.

What happened? Why did he start breaking my heart? Why did he decide to go on that trip with his colleagues when it was our second anniversary and he knew I wanted us to be together? Why did he tell me two years ago that he never really enjoyed his time with me that day when I got angry with him? Didn't he really enjoy his time with me?

Did he really not love me in the first place, and I have been living in an illusion thinking we were madly in love? Was he lying when he once told me that I was the best thing that happened in his life? Was he lying when he told me that he didn't know what love is until he met me? Why did he . . . ?

When our first daughter was born and I wasn't sleeping for weeks and I was counting on him to be there with me, he went to that party at his friend's house although I told him not to go. He didn't care about me anymore. He only wanted me while I was attractive and energetic and fun. But as soon as I got busy with the kids he distanced himself from me. I wish I hadn't made all those sacrifices for him. I made his life. I was a loving wife to him and a friend who always comforted him, encouraged him, and supported him to have the success that he has now.

But he always put me down. Maybe he is jealous I am a smart, successful, beautiful woman. And he tried to push me down on purpose. What if he never really loved me and he used me to be his comfort and his support for his own personal success?

I lost the best years of my life. I am a smart successful woman. I deserve better than this.

Does he really love me? Why after all the things that I have done for him, did he still treat me the way he did? Maybe I wasn't really enough to be loved. Maybe I am not worthy. Otherwise why would he behave like that while I was doing all these things for him?

Yes, that's it. I'm not worthy.

Sarah is going down a spiral of negative thinking and making assumptions, most of which are probably not true. She is revisiting her perceptions and conclusions about some of the events in her life and painting them with a negative brush.

Sarah realizes that she wants happiness, but she is not happy. She feels lack: lack of love, lack of support, lack of fulfillment. And so she starts looking for why she feels this way. Her mind leads her to the easiest explanation: "It is Alan's fault that I'm not happy."

She falls victim to the mind's natural tendency to put the blame on someone else.

She takes herself out of the equation. Her mind convinces her that she has good reasons to feel depressed and unhappy. It also offers her all sorts of reasons for why all those things happened to her and why she was treated the way she was. Based on these reasons, many of which could be exaggerations and are unfounded, she came to the conclusion that she was not worthy.

Now, let's look at a different way Sarah's thoughts could have unfolded.

Scenario 2:

She thinks: Why am I feeling like this now? I am sitting here on this beautiful afternoon, watching my kids playing happily with their father, and I am relaxing and reading, sipping my tea. Look at my daughters, how happy and joyful they are. I'm proud of myself for being such a good mom and raising such happy, healthy, and joyful children.

And it is so good that Alan is a really diligent father. He makes sure he spends time with the kids and he plays with them and makes them feel loved and cared for. And he is loving and supportive to me most of the time, too.

Why don't I feel happy? What is wrong in my life that I don't feel joy and I feel depressed? I am a successful woman, who has used my life well. I wanted to become a medical doctor and I am. I met the love of my life whom I always believed was my soulmate. We spent many years in a beautiful relationship, being happy and joyful together, and we still love each other and enjoy each other's company. We both worked hard for our successes and we supported each other.

And look at us now. We have two beautiful healthy, happy daughters, a nice comfortable home, and a good relationship. Really, what is preventing me from feeling relaxed and happy?

Oh, Alan broke my heart seven years ago when I desperately needed him that night when our daughter was sick and she was crying all day and I told Alan not to go to that party at his friend's house and begged him to stay at home and look after our daughter. I was so tired, I needed some sleep. But he left anyway. I still feel heartbroken when I remember that night. It makes my heart sink just considering that maybe I was not really that important for him as much as I thought I was.

But is that really true? Maybe I am exaggerating. He should have stayed. But most of the time, he was with me, supporting me, helping me, comforting me, looking after the kids. There were many times that I felt so blessed that I had him and he made me feel the most important creature on earth. He was good most of the times and sometimes he was not as good as I expected and he was selfish. But I was selfish sometimes, too. He is not perfect. But neither am I. No one is perfect.

Look at us now. We passed through all the ups and downs and now here we are. We still love each other. Our daughters get to be raised by two caring, loving parents in a comfortable home and a relaxed atmosphere. I know many people who have a lot of tension in their relationships and their children are growing up in a tense environment. But we are relaxed with each other. I feel blessed.

Maybe I am making myself too busy. Maybe I am not spending enough time relaxing and enjoying all the beautiful things that I have created. I deserve all these things and I worked hard to have them and to keep them in my life. Maybe I need a little bit more time off for myself to enjoy all these things that I have created in my life and worked for.

Maybe I should start playing piano again. Oh, how I love playing. And how I miss playing. I've been neglecting my passion for music.

Maybe I should love myself more. I am too hard on myself. I work hard to achieve what I want. But once I get there I don't take time to appreciate and enjoy my accomplishments. I'm always on the go. I place high expectations on myself. I should be kinder to myself. I should take more time for myself and enjoy my life more. I should be proud of myself for what I have created in my life, for being a good mother to my children, a loving wife to my husband, a caring doctor to my patients, a trustworthy confidant to my friends.

I am proud of myself. I am enough. Life is good.

I need to spend more time on myself and enjoy my life.

In scenario 2, Sarah challenges her negative thoughts and starts to look at her situation in a broader way, seeing more aspects to her situation. Sure enough, she finds many good things that are in her life. And she realizes that she hasn't been spending enough time recognizing, appreciating, and enjoying them.

Taking a broader view, she doesn't fall into the automatic mode of her mind that exaggerates the negatives while neglecting the positives.

In conscious mode, she finds what might be blocking her joy and explores what she can do to start enjoying her life more.

Sarah has a choice between these two scenarios. In fact, Sarah has many scenarios to choose from. The scenario she chooses will have an impact on her life—on her decisions, on her feelings, on how she views herself and the world around her, and how she experiences her life.

Her choice will alter her life and its direction.

In scenario 1, Sarah doesn't think she has a choice. But that makes her a victim to the automatic unconscious thought process that is happening in her mind. She does have a choice. One of her other choices is scenario 2.

> What we feel inside us is not determined by our circumstances, but it is determined by *what we think* about our circumstances. And that thinking is a choice. It is not a question of having a choice but of how to use it.

In scenario 2, Sarah has more control over the thoughts in her mind. She challenges her negative thoughts and looks consciously to see if she has other options. She chooses to view the situation from other angles, too, instead of automatically and unknowingly believing in every thought that comes to her mind. She does not fall victim to her own mind.

If Sarah is in the habit of falling victim to her mind and *unconsciously* chooses scenarios similar to scenario 1 quite often, she repeatedly creates toxic emotions in her body that over a period of time can affect her health. Living in survival mode much of the time also affects her self-esteem, her sense of worth, how she interacts with her husband and her kids, and the story that she tells herself about her life.

Much of Sarah's pain could be avoided if she decided not to fall victim to the automatic process of her mind and to challenge her negative thoughts by questioning them and looking at the situations from different angles before falling into hasty conclusions.

In short, most of her pain could be avoided by choosing her thoughts consciously.

At each moment, we also have many scenarios to choose from in our minds. The judgments we make about ourselves and others and about our life situations and life itself, the thoughts and memories we choose to hold on to or let go of, the dreams we choose to have about our future, and everything that we choose in each moment are choices that we make either consciously or unconsciously. They impact us whether or not we realize it.

> You have the ability to create happiness inside yourself regardless of your outside situation the same way you can create feelings of sadness and anxiety regardless of your external circumstances— by thought and imagination alone. Happiness is a conscious choice you can make every day.

The Benefits of the *Make Conscious Choices* Technique

As human beings, we are the only species that can choose what to think and how to feel. Taking advantage of this special ability can bring us freedom over how we experience life.

We might think that our feelings are the consequences of our circumstances. However, masters of wisdom say that what we feel inside us is not determined by our circumstances, but it is determined by *what we think* about our circumstances.

And that thinking is a choice.

It is not a question of having a choice but of how to use it.

Even happiness is a choice. We can consciously choose to be happy instead of living by default.

Today's fast-paced world frequently triggers our survival mode, making us live by default most of the time. It is important to remind ourselves that we have a choice and to practice our choices.

When we are feeling stressed, our brains think that we are not safe. In such instances, we can choose to shift to conscious mode and make conscious choices. In conscious mode, we can choose what we want to think, what we want to feel, and what we want to do.

You can choose to be happy and look for ways to create the feeling of happiness inside you without being dependent on other people or external circumstances to make you happy. You have the ability to create happiness inside yourself regardless of your outside situation the same way you can create feelings of sadness and anxiety regardless of your external circumstances—by thought and imagination alone.

Happiness is a conscious choice you can make every day.

How to Do the *Make Conscious Choices* Technique

To put your conscious choices into practice, you can start by making at least one conscious choice every day. Make that conscious choice as soon as you wake up to set the tone for your day.

Before you get out of bed and start your day:

Step 1: *Remember that you have a choice.*

Remind yourself that you have a choice about how you want to feel.

For example, remind yourself of the following truths:

> "I can choose to be happy today, or I can choose to be
> unhappy today."
> "I can choose to enjoy today, or I can choose not to enjoy
> today."
> "I can choose to feel good today, or I can choose not to feel
> good today."

Step 2: *Ask about your choices.*

Ask yourself which way you want to choose.

> "Which way do I *want* to choose to feel today?"

Step 3: *Make your choice.*

Make your choice and speak your choice in your mind.

> "I choose to be happy today."
> "I choose to enjoy today."
> "I choose to feel good today."

You can practice your choice during the day as well. During the day, remind yourself of the choice you made in the morning, and act based on this choice as much as possible.

If you choose to be happy today, you can smile when you remember this choice. Or you can notice what thoughts are marching around in your mind and examine whether they are positive or negative. If they are negative, you can interrupt the pattern of the negative thoughts and consciously think of some positive thoughts that make you happy—thoughts of a happy memory, thoughts of the blessings that you have in your life today, thoughts of a desired future that you are working to build.

Or when you start to feel stressed, you can immediately follow the 3 steps above and remind yourself of your choices and make a choice that you want, instead of letting your mind automatically react to the situation. Make your choice and see what you can do to create the positive feeling that you have chosen.

For example, if someone insults you, you can immediately remind yourself, "I can choose to enjoy today, or I can choose to let this ruin the rest of my day. Which one do I *want* to choose?" And if you find that you really want to enjoy your day, then consider how you can respond to this insult so that you can still enjoy your day in spite of it.

Or if you feel physical pain during the day, you can remind yourself that you have a choice and follow the steps above.

Remind yourself that you can choose to focus on the pain and how terrible it is and how it is making your life uncomfortable. Or you can choose to have a positive emotion and look for ways to heal the pain or to be with it peacefully if you cannot heal it.

See if you can smile in spite of this pain. See if you can do any of the strategies in this book to help you heal the pain. See if you can feel grateful for the good things that you have in your life in spite of this pain. See if this pain is a messenger that is showing you something that you are doing wrong or ignoring in your life.

One thing to consider while making your choices is to step back from the situation for a moment and look at it from a point in the future. Jump ahead ten or twenty years from now, or even at the moment you are taking your last breath.

Which choice would you want your past self to have made? Would you regret choosing to be happy or unhappy? Would you have wished to have chosen to enjoy your day instead of allowing a problem to ruin it?

In the book *The Top Five Regrets of the Dying*, Bronnie Ware mentions that one of the top five regrets of the people who are near their death is "I wish that I had let myself be happier."[30]

We can learn from these people who are going through the most precious moments of their lives—the last ones—and we can live their lesson: To let ourselves be happier.

At each moment, we have a choice to choose happiness and to live the life that is true to ourselves, a life that we genuinely want to live. The question is, "Do we make these choices consciously?"

The *Make Conscious Choices* Technique in Action

Maggie's story in an inspiring example of how the Make Conscious Choices technique can help us focus on and create what we want.

Maggie is the daughter of one of my meditation students. She recently graduated from university and found a job. She is an engineer and a smart girl. However, she wasn't comfortable with the politics at work. She didn't like the gossiping and backbiting among her coworkers. But she really resented her workload. She felt she was doing the amount of work of three people and the only one staying late. She also saw her colleagues getting credit for the work she had done.

She was feeling so much stress that it started to affect her physical and mental health. She became increasingly anxious and forgetful and her heart would race. As a birthday gift to Maggie, her mother signed her up for my G.R.O.W. program to lower her stress.

At first, she saw herself trapped in her problems at work. She couldn't stand the toxic environment but couldn't leave either.

What if she finds another job and the next job is also like this one or even worse? She was living in fear and not doing anything to make her situation better.

The turning point came when she started getting clarity about what she wants and what she doesn't want. She let her fear take a break and she let herself take a break from fear. She began to understand that a new job may or may not have better working conditions. She doesn't know yet. But she does know that her current situation (that she doesn't like) will continue as long as she doesn't make a change.

I asked her to do an experiment and see what happens. Her assignment was to focus on what she wants, which was another job, instead of getting lost in her problems at work and focusing on what she doesn't want. And to do that she agreed to consciously choose to think of her goal and remind herself first thing in the morning and then over and over again during the day that her goal is to find another job and she will spend her energy looking for a new job.

This helped her stay more in control of her emotions. When things bothered her at work, she would focus on the fact that she will go home and search for another job and soon she will be out of this situation.

Just consciously choosing what she wants to focus on (instead of letting her mind wander in the automatic negative thinking) helped her become calmer. And at nights she would search for new jobs and apply for the jobs she liked.

Maggie sent out seventeen job applications in two weeks. In those two weeks she was so focused on this project of finding a new job that she almost forgot her problems at work. She realized that soon she will be leaving that environment and it's a waste of time to keep thinking about what her colleagues are saying or doing.

But after two weeks, when she ran out of new jobs to apply for and hadn't heard back about any of the applications she'd already sent, she started losing hope and fear began to creep back into her mind. She needed a little bit of encouragement to continue her experiment and make conscious choices.

I reminded her that she had found her current job and she could find another one. I told her that the more applications she sends, the more likely it is she'll find another job. And I said that if she doesn't find any new jobs to apply for she could follow-up on the applications she'd already submitted. One week later, she told me this exciting news: she had two job interviews. There was no sign of stress, anxiety, or hopelessness in her anymore.

> You have only one life chance, and you deserve to think and feel the way you want in this precious life. When you live in conscious mode and make conscious choices, you take responsibility for the content of your mind and how you experience your life.

As challenging as it was, Maggie did not let survival mode get the best of her. Instead she made conscious choices to get the result she wanted.

Now she knows that when she faces a problem or wants to grow her life, she can choose the thoughts that serve her best, then act based on those thoughts to unlock the life she wants.

The Significance of the *Make Conscious Choices* Technique

We make choices all day long. Most of the time we do so unconsciously because our brain tends to default to autopilot. But our choices, whether they are conscious or unconscious, affect our lives.

We don't have to believe and follow every thought that our mind brings. By making conscious choices, we shift from the autopilot mode to the conscious mode. We can then take control of our decisions and our actions and how we perceive our life situations and experience life.

You have only one life chance, and you deserve to think and feel the way you want in this precious life. When you live in conscious mode and make conscious choices, you take responsibility for the content of your mind and how you experience your life. You have the ability to achieve your dreams and be happier while you do so. By consciously choosing to have positive thoughts and positive emotions, you choose a happy mind—and a happy mind is healing.

CHAPTER 8

EMPHASIZE THE POSITIVE

EARLY ONE SUMMER, my husband and I traveled to the UK to attend a master class and retreat held by my meditation teacher, Vikas Malkani, and to do some sightseeing. It was an amazing trip full of wonderful moments. We enjoyed hiking, visiting different cities and villages, seeing new places, trying local foods, and meeting new people.

On the last two days of the trip we stayed in London. The first day was beautiful and sunny. We were through Hyde Park and then throughout the city. Every time we considered taking a taxi, we chose to walk instead and enjoy the beautiful weather.

By the end of the day, we'd walked more than thirteen miles. My legs and feet were very tired. Back at the hotel, I sat on the bed and stretched my legs. You can imagine how good that felt!

Stretching my legs presented the perfect opportunity to practice one of my strategies for training my mind to stay positive. I call it the *Emphasize the Positive*[31] technique.

I have a *word* that I say whenever I have an experience that makes me feel good. From small moments of pleasant experience to big events, I notice them and say my designated word to emphasize each happening and make them more stand out in my mind.

Feeling the relief in my legs after a whole day of walking felt good, so I said my word while paying attention to the ease spreading through my muscles.

The Emphasize the Positive technique is an extremely simple strategy that I frequently use on a daily basis to keep my mind positive and train it to notice positives experiences.

Emphasize the Positive Experience

We usually have a word or a few choice words that we say when we encounter something we don't like or when we have a negative experience. But I have a word that I use when I encounter something that I like and makes me feel good.

This technique was inspired by Persian culture. In Persian culture, there is a specific word that people say when they want to express their enjoyment or satisfaction of a situation. The Persian word is *aakheysh*. It doesn't have a specific meaning. It's more an interjection to express a joyful moment.

For example, when I was growing up, I'd hear my dad say *aakheysh* when he came home at noon for lunch during a summer day and he'd drink a cold glass of water. Or I'd hear my mom say *aakheysh* when she sat down on chair when she was tired. Or I'd hear my grandma say *aakheysh* when she kissed her grandchildren.

One day after I moved to Australia, I had an aha moment. I had been contemplating the importance of having positive thoughts and that by default our minds tend to spend more time in survival mode and to focus on negative experiences.

It occurred to me that this expression from the Persian culture could be turned into a conscious practice to train the mind to notice the positive moments that we experience throughout the day.

Since then I've used this strategy. I say my *word*— "*Aakheysh!*"—whenever I feel good to emphasize the good experience in my mind.

It feels good to sit down on the sofa after a long, tiring day. I notice the good feeling and I say my word. It feels good to take a bite of a ripe, juicy fruit. I notice the good feeling and I say my word. It feels good to take a sip of hot tea. I notice the good feeling and I say my *word*.

Saying my word helps me capture the pleasant moments and notice the positive experiences that my mind would have otherwise automatically overlooked and ignored. Paying attention to these moments brings more flavor to my days. At the same time, it trains my mind to see the positive experiences instead of passing through them without giving them any importance.

In spite of its utter simplicity, this technique helps you go beyond survival mode to become more conscious of the good moments in your life and gradually strengthen your happy muscles.

The way Persians celebrate the arrival of spring and the new year is another aspect of the culture that inspires me to emphasize positive feelings and train my mind to notice them.

Persian new year is the first day of spring, called Nowruz, which means "the new day." Nowruz celebrations last for thirteen days. It is the most important celebration in Iran and dates back more than three thousand years. It celebrates the arrival of spring when light and warmth come to take away the darkness and coldness of winter. With spring, nature wakes up from a long sleep, and earth comes to life again. Nowruz doesn't just recognize the change of season; it recognizes the renewal of the earth and a new cycle of life beginning. It marks a fresh start, a new year, and a time to celebrate.

Nowruz is the happiest time of the year in Iran. As a child I noticed how everyone's mood lightened and lifted in the weeks leading up to Nowruz.

People start spring cleaning, they buy new clothes, and they buy nuts and sweets to offer to guests who come to visit them during the holiday.

There are many Persian poems about how the coming of spring and blossoming of flowers invites celebration and joy.

The following is a poem by Hafiz, whose poetry is found in every home in Iran.

> Spring and all its flowers
> now joyously break their vow of silence.
> It is time for celebration, not for lying low;
> You too—weed out those roots of sadness from your heart.
>
> —Translated by Homayun Taba and Marguerite Theophil

Prior to Nowruz, people decorate a table called a haft-seen, or Seven S's, table. On the table is a collection of seven objects whose names in Farsi all start with the letter *S* and symbolize good wishes for the new year. Usually the seven items are sprouted wheat, an apple, vinegar, *samanu* (a sweet pudding made with sprouted wheat), garlic, sumac (a spice made from the dried berries of the sumac bush), and *senjed* (a dried fruit known as silverberry). These items symbolize love, health, wisdom, prosperity, and other things people wish for in the new year.

A few minutes before the old year makes way for the new year, the family gathers around the haft-seen table in their new clothes. Everyone sits silently while listening to the countdown to the new year on the television or radio. The moment the countdown finishes and the new year arrives, everyone rejoices and kisses each other. As a symbol of a new start, parents give new banknotes to children as gifts.

In my family, soon after the new year arrived, we'd go to my grandmother's house. For the next thirteen days, we'd visit relatives. We'd play, talk, laugh, eat sweets, nuts, and seeds, such as pistachios, almonds, peanuts, roasted pumpkin seeds, and Jabani seeds (the seed of an inedible watermelon grown in a village in the northern part of Iran), and drink black tea. When we would leave, our hosts would give me and the other guests' children new banknotes.

> When you make a practice of emphasizing your positive experiences, you will notice that you can find such moments in your everyday life, even when you are going through difficult times. You can always choose to emphasize a positive experience, no matter how brief it may be.

These happy memories of celebrating spring touched me deeply and made celebrating every positive life experience a conscious practice for me many years later, after I understood the wisdom behind it.

When you make a practice of emphasizing your positive experiences, you will notice that you can find such moments in your everyday life, even when you are going through difficult times. You can always choose to emphasize a positive experience, no matter how brief it may be.

You Can Find the Positive Even in Times of Catastrophe

After Japan's 2011 Tōhoku earthquake and tsunami, we didn't have electricity, water, or gas for several days. Most of our meals were cold, bread and biscuits, but a few times my husband and I managed to cook noodles over a candle flame. We appreciated those simple, warm meals. I still remember how good it felt to eat those modest meals together.

I will also never forget a meal we had with our neighbors.

Four days after the earthquake, our neighbors gathered in an open space in front of the community center and started a fire. They brought a big cauldron. Everyone contributed whatever they had at home: noodles, mushrooms, potatoes, carrots, sauces, single-use bowls. They made a warm soup and everyone shared the meal.

That day, despite the overwhelming experience of the earthquake and the tsunami, the sadness over the lives that were lost, and the uncertainty of the aftershocks of this disaster, a sense of peace was present during the preparation and sharing of this meal.

The neighborhood created a meaningful and memorable moment by fostering a sense of connection and sharing. It was a small bowl of soup for everyone, but the love in that small bowl of soup was nourishment for the soul as well as the body.

Sipping my warm bowl of soup, I said aakheysh out of habit from my Persian culture. At that time I hadn't made saying aakheysh a conscious practice yet. But I said it to express the good feeling of a warm meal with my neighbors, and, more important, the wonderful feeling of being present at such a powerful moment of human connection in such a catastrophic situation.

No matter how difficult life may get at times, we can still find positive experiences to focus on.

This experience taught me another lesson that is worth mentioning here. I had not expected the sense of peace that pervaded the preparation and sharing of the meal. It was so prominent that it was almost impossible to miss. It took some time and thought for me to understand it.

Here's what I realized: *We carry the ability to experience peace at all times.*

The world around us may be full of chaos, but we always have a sense of peace inside us ready to be tapped.

Sometimes a shock, like the shock of a natural disaster or other unexpected event, throws us into that valley of peace. A shock is like a pause, a sudden disruption of a pattern. And that abrupt disruption may shut down our normal routine way of reacting and throw us into a different state of mind in which that state of peace is available.

The point here is not that we should look forward to such a shock. We should not. The point is that we are capable of experiencing this sense of peace at any time. We can visit this space consciously if we know how.

The question is, how can we find a way to consciously visit that space of peace inside us?

When our mind is busy with the endless day-to-day activities in our fast-paced lives, we don't have time to pause and relax, to open the door and enter that peaceful space inside us.

If we learn how to pause and consciously bring our mind to a state of relaxation, we can access the deeper spaces in our mind where this sense of peace and other positive emotions reside.

By introducing pauses and reducing speed, we help our mind to shift from survival mode to conscious mode.

Noticing our positive emotions and focusing on them is an easy way to make this shift. And when we look for them, we can find them even in the most catastrophic times. If we choose to look, we can always find positive experiences to focus on.

The Emphasize the Positive technique is one way to do that. Choose a word that will become a symbol of positive feelings for you, and you can say your word when you notice a good feeling that you are already experiencing.

You can define a word or create a word for yourself and use it as a tool to emphasize your positive experiences. The word can be in any language. It doesn't have to have a meaning. And it doesn't have to make sense. It's an exclamation. It's an interjection. It's a word that expresses an emotion, similar to *wow, oops, aw,* and *aha.* But it's a word that you connect to a positive feeling or experience.

In the following section I will explain why this simple technique works.

Negativity Bias

Throughout the day, we experience many good moments, and at times maybe some not very good moments. However, at the end of the day, we are more likely to remember the negative experiences rather than the positive ones. We talk to different people and hear many friendly words and compliments, and sometimes maybe a couple of criticisms. But one criticism can wash away the many positive sentiments that we heard. The criticism stays with us for the rest of the day or maybe even for days or weeks.

For the sake of survival, it is the mind's natural tendency to ignore the positive and emphasize the negative. But research shows that this affects how we think, feel, and act, and it influences our decisions, behaviors, and relationships.[32,33,34] There is an asymmetry between how our brain handles our negative experiences and how it handles our positive experiences. Psychologists call this "positive-negative asymmetry," or "the negativity bias." This comes from the time of our ancestors.

Imagine our ancestors coming out of their cave and seeing a hungry tiger and a beautiful flower. Which one should they pay attention to? Paying attention to the tiger will save their lives. So, our tendency to focus on the negative, our negativity bias, is a survival mechanism that was effective at saving the lives of our ancestors. We are living with the same brain that our ancestors did. And this negativity bias still plays a role in our survival but it does not need to play the dominant role.

We don't see tigers in our day-to-day life. We have few life-and-death moments. But our brains don't know that. They sense our modern-day stresses as tigers. New emails in our mailbox, getting stuck in the traffic, or dealing with uncertainties make our brains feel threatened all day long. And when our brains are threatened they default to survival mode and negativity bias.

Our minds magnify negative experiences, making them appear more important than they really are.

If we live by default, we will function based on the survival mode. And we miss many of the beautiful experiences that we have during the day: the beautiful flowers in the florist's window or the good feeling of having a bite of our favorite meal or a sip of our favorite drink.

If we want to be happy, heal our pain, and go beyond survival to thrive, we need to function in conscious mode, not survival mode. It's our job to make the switch happen.

The Benefits of the *Emphasize the Positive* Technique

The Emphasize the Positive technique is another strategy to shift your brain from survival mode to conscious mode.

With this technique, we consciously choose where we want to put our attention. We practice noticing and emphasizing our positive experiences to train our minds to learn to notice our positive experiences instead of ignoring them. This addresses the positive-negative asymmetry and gradually evens out the balance between the positive and the negative in your mind.

Normally, we have plenty of positive experiences in a given day. Negative experiences are usually occasional. They might happen every now and then. But when we live by the default mode, our survival brain ignores our positive experiences, so we don't notice most of the good experiences that we have. Ignoring our positive experiences then becomes a habit.

If you practice paying attention to your positive experiences, sure enough you will develop the habit of noticing more of the positive aspects of your life.

The more you pay attention to the positive, the stronger your awareness of the positive will grow. And the more you pay attention to the negative, the stronger your awareness of the negative will grow.

Paying attention to the positives instead of ignoring them and exaggerating the negatives trains your mind to see the whole of life as it is, in the correct proportion. You'll see what is actually taking place in the present moment and not overlook the positive elements.

If you develop the ability to see positives and negatives in the correct proportion, then gradually you will be able to see your experiences in proportion. Problems, difficulties, and pain have a place but they won't take up more space than they need to.

When you see life from a wider angle, you are more likely to do something about your pain, whether it's in your body or in your mind. You may look deeper to find what is causing this pain. You may consider what you did or thought that caused this pain in the first place and correct that if you are still doing it.

At times, you may even forget your pain if you are fully engaged in all the good things that are happening in your moments.

When you learn to see the whole as it is, with positives as well as negatives, instead of being trapped by the negatives and ignoring the positives things, you live more consciously. You are able to make conscious choices and act based on your best ability and for your best future.

Paying attention to the positives instead of ignoring them and exaggerating the negatives trains your mind to see the whole of life as it is, in the correct proportion. You'll see what is actually taking place in the present moment and not overlook the positive elements.

Besides, you allow yourself to relax and provide more opportunities for your mind throughout the day to connect with the sense of peace within you.

Another benefit of the Emphasize the Positive technique is that your designated word becomes a trigger for positive feelings. The mind learns that this *word* represents a positive *feeling*. The word and the feeling become the two ends of the same thread. By bringing out any of these two ends, you bring out the thread, and therefore the other end. In other words, it works from both sides.

When you start using this practice, first you will have a positive feeling, and then you will say your word to acknowledge it. Gradually your mind will associate this *word* with a positive *feeling*. Once the mind makes that connection, the technique works two ways. Now, just by saying your word, you can trigger the positive feeling associated with it.

How to Do the *Emphasize the Positive* Technique

With the Emphasize the Positive technique, you will practice noticing your positive experiences and emphasizing them by assigning a word to them.

First, choose a word that feels natural for you to say when you want to express a good feeling. It can be a sound, a word that exists, or a word that you make up. For example: Yes. Haaaah. Yay. Aah.

Step 1: *Notice the good experience.*

Whenever you have a good experience, notice it.

Step 2: *Say your word.*

Say your word to emphasize that experience in your mind.

Step 3: *Pay attention to the positive experience.*

As you say your word, pay conscious attention to the good feeling the positive experience causes in you and take a moment to fully feel and enjoy it.

When you experience any good feeling, big or small, notice it, emphasize it by saying your word, and take a moment to pay attention and enjoy it. Good feelings may arise after a big victory, when you drink a refreshing glass of water, or even when you are sitting quietly.

I encourage you to make a conscious choice in the morning to notice your positive experiences throughout the day and emphasize them. With practice over time, you will become aware of many more positive experiences throughout your day that you hadn't noticed before.

The *Emphasize the Positive* Technique in Action

Claire practiced Emphasize the Positive technique to help her navigate the tough times during her divorce. I was introduced to Claire at a party at a friend's house in Sydney and we met up a few times after that.

One day, I casually told her about the concept behind the Emphasize the Positive technique, even though I hadn't chosen a name for this technique yet. I shared how fascinated I was that such simple habits, could create such big impacts in our lives.

Almost a year later, Claire broke the news to me that she was going through a divorce. During this difficult time, she remembered what I'd said about emphasizing positive experiences and decided to give it a try. She started looking for any positive experience in her day to emphasize.

Although at first she thought there were no positive experiences, with practice, she noticed she could find some if she looked for them. Drinking her coffee in the morning or soaking in a bath were positive experiences that made her feel good, and she chose to emphasize them by noting them and saying her word—"*Aaaah*." The more she practiced, the more she realized how many good experiences fill her days, even the bad days, and she can find them when she makes an intention to find them.

This practice made her feel good. At first, just for a moment, but eventually the good feeling spread throughout her day.

It also helped her realize how she had been completely ignoring those short moments of positivity before, and therefore had been missing out on the positive feelings that could help her cope better with her dark moments and make her good days happier as well.

The Significance of the *Emphasize the Positive* Technique

Instead of living with the unconscious habit of seeing the negatives, a product of your survival instinct, you can consciously choose to see the positives and live in conscious, healing mode.

Just as our survival brain made the habit of giving importance to the negatives by noticing our negative experiences and paying attention to them, in the Emphasize the Positive technique we use the same laws of nature to create a habit of giving importance to the positives. We consciously notice the positive experiences in our lives and pay attention to them.

The Emphasize the Positive technique is a tool to train your brain to switch from survival mode to conscious mode, see the positives and negatives in life in more realistic proportion, appreciate the many good experiences you encounter in every moment of your life, and enjoy their blessings. You'll train your mind to notice the good experiences that are already present in your life, experiences that by default you haven't learned to notice and your mind tends to ignore.

> Just as our survival brain made the habit of giving importance to the negatives by noticing our negative experiences and paying attention to them, in the Emphasize the Positive technique we use the same laws of nature to create a habit of giving importance to the positives.

This also brings a pause in your mind to make the peace inside you more accessible to you.

Moreover, your word becomes a trigger for your mind to initiate positive feelings in your heart and healing chemicals in your body. With this simple training, you exercise the happy muscles of your brain and move toward a happy mind that heals your pain.

CHAPTER 9

DESIGN YOUR BEST FUTURE

DURING SUMMER BREAK, when I was nine years old, my parents sent me to a painting class. The teacher was a young lady who had just graduated from university and had started classes in her father's workshop. Her father was my calligraphy teacher.

One day in class, my painting teacher told us, "Draw your dream. Draw what you dream of."

I thought for a moment. I didn't know what I dreamed of. I couldn't think of anything I would change or wish to have. Everything was perfect as it was. But then suddenly an idea came to me.

I picked up my pencil and started drawing a bird. I drew my head as its head and then the body of a bird. Its wings were wide open and it was flying high in the sky. Below the bird, I drew trees, mountains, and a river. I finished my sketch and then painted it in vibrant colors.

When I showed my painting to the teacher, she said, "Do you want to be a bird?"

I said, "I want to be free."

This was a strange longing for a nine-year-old child who was full of happiness and joy. But this dream was vivid. I imagined how a bird feels free when it opens its wings and glides on the air. I imagined that I could go farther and faster if I could fly instead of walk. I imagined how much of the ground I could see from high in the sky. This painting captures the feelings of freedom and limitlessness I dreamed of.

When my hands started sketching that bird, they were showing me what I truly wanted in life.

I wanted to expand. I wanted to grow. I wanted to know. I wanted to reach my highest potential. I wanted to be free.

It wasn't until twenty-six years later that I found the wisdom that brings freedom—inner freedom.

And it wasn't until thirty-two years later, when I was going through the treatments for Lyme disease, that I remembered my painting teacher and that painting.

During those treatments, one of my strategies to stay calm and pay attention to the positives was to keep focus on my happy, healthy, energetic future self. I would imagine my future self pain-free, doing all the activities I love to do and fulfilling her dreams. I saw myself writing my first book—this book—giving talks and speeches to large audiences, teaching, coaching, touching lives, and feeling joyful.

One day I saw a TEDx talk named *Draw Your Future*.[35] While I was watching the video, I suddenly remembered that day in my painting class.

Putting this together with what I knew now about the power of our minds to create our lives, I realized my painting teacher was teaching us a powerful technique that day. Immediately I picked up a journal and started to draw what I dreamed for my best future (what I was seeing in my imagination every day). And I loved it. I decided to draw my future self every day in addition to visualizing it to emphasize my best future in my mind and help it hold this picture of my future and my dream more easily.

After that, every day after I had my breakfast and before I started work, I'd pick up my journal, sit on the sofa, and imagine my best future. Though my body or mind was in pain, I would focus on this future with a feeling of joy. I'd sketch a picture of myself in my best future—living the life of my dreams, fulfilling my life's purpose, feeling happy and joyful. And then I'd color it. Imagining how many people my work would touch, how many lives it would change, and how much pain it would heal was a fuel that fed the fire of my passion to create this future to help myself and others.

When our bodies or minds are going through discomfort, it is easier for us to let go of our dreams and live lives that are less than what we deserve and desire. However, by stepping up and choosing to keep our dreams alive, despite the temporary difficulty, we get closer to the future we want.

One day, shortly after I started this practice, I was feeling pumped with good feelings for my best future, and I started to sing about how I was going to feel in the future I was imagining and drawing. It felt good. I realized this could be another way to emphasize my imagined future in my mind.

And the *Design Your Best Future*[36] technique was born.

Every day since that day, I'd imagine and draw my best future. Then I'd sing my feelings about what I am doing in this best future and what I am feeling while I am experiencing it. I'd improvise the melody and lyrics, singing about whatever I wanted to do as my healthiest self in that moment.

Imagining, drawing, and singing about my future self would shift my mind from any discomfort I was feeling and inspire me to do whatever I could at that moment to make the best use of my day and get closer to manifesting that future. It worked wonderfully to help me remember my goal and my intention over and over again during the day and to stay positive, peaceful, and purposeful.

It strengthened me, empowering me to feel responsible and in charge of my life and how I experience it and not become a victim of my illness.

Focus on the Best

When our bodies or minds are going through discomfort, it is easier for us to let go of our dreams and live lives that are less than what we deserve and desire. However, by stepping up and choosing to keep our dreams alive, despite the temporary difficulty, we get closer to the future we want.

It is especially critical to take ourselves to the zone of happiness and purpose when we are going through difficulties. If we let our minds react automatically to unwanted events, they will work based on survival mode and focus on all of the negatives, causing us worry and anxiety. This prevents us from living the lives we want and causes our future to be less than it can be.

That's why it is important to shift to conscious mode and remind ourselves of our goals. Every day. Remember, the mind's natural tendency is to get distracted. It needs discipline to keep its focus on our purpose.

Whether life is going smoothly or challenging us, we need the tools to help us keep our focus on our dreams and empower us to take small steps to fulfill them.

> When we set the destination for our minds, our minds work to bring us more creative ways to manifest our goals. We get clear about the steps we need to take to reach our destination. And we are more inspired to take those steps.

Focus helps our brains find ways to make our dreams happen.

It is rewarding to be conscious and to give our minds a specific and clear destination. When we set the destination for our minds, our minds work to bring us more creative ways to manifest our goals. We get clear about the steps we need to take to reach our destination. And we are more inspired to take those steps.

It does not matter how small a step we take; what matters is that we remain focused on our goal and move in that direction as much or as little as possible. It is the progress toward the goal that counts, not the size of the step we take.

This reminds me of a fable many of us heard as children: the story of the tortoise and the hare running a race. Although the hare is much faster than the tortoise, he doesn't win the race. The hare runs fast at the beginning, but then he gets tired and stops running and takes a nap. He thinks to himself that he will win the race regardless because he runs so fast. The tortoise is much slower than the hare, but he takes one step after another, consistently and persistently, and eventually wins the race.

We don't have to take big steps to progress toward our goals. All we need is to keep our minds focused on our destination and take small steps consistently and persistently to reach it.

To live a life of purpose and fulfillment and unlock the life we want, we must be conscious as often as possible and see where we are heading. We can choose the best future consciously and strive to move toward it. We can choose, as Rumi says, to "let the beauty we love be what we do."

Your best future consists of what you love to do and what you enjoy rather that what you don't like. You have the capacity to imagine it and even create it. When you focus on what you love to do, you enter your creative zone. It makes you expand. It makes you grow.

> To live a life of purpose and fulfillment and unlock the life we want, we must be conscious as often as possible and see where we are heading. We can choose the best future consciously and strive to move toward it.

When you do the work that you love—the work that gives you joy—this joy changes the chemistry in your body to make you healthier, stronger, and more creative.

In life, even if you are facing challenges or uncertainties, find the work that you enjoy doing, imagine your best future, hold your focus on that best future, and do whatever you can in the moment to bring that future closer. This will smooth your journey, bring joy to your moments, help heal your pain, and get you closer to what you desire.

If the road of life is bumpy sometimes, you need to be more conscious to stay focused on your destination. The bumps may slow your journey, but by remaining conscious you can continue to move forward and still enjoy the ride.

You might need to slow down or rest. But you can always keep the vision and the intention active in your mind.

Consistently seeing, planning, and working toward your best future while you are relaxed in the gifts of the present moment elevates your mood and makes you feel good. This makes your brain more creative and empowers you with better equipment to create that future.

The Design Your Best Future technique will show you how to consciously focus on your future.

> In life, even if you are facing challenges or uncertainties, find the work that you enjoy doing, imagine your best future, hold your focus on that best future, and do whatever you can in the moment to bring that future closer.

The Benefits of the *Design Your Best Future* Technique

The trinity of Imagine, Draw, Sing is an effective strategy to keep your focus on your purpose and design your best future.

This is a powerful tool to shift your focus away from the automatic negative thoughts associated with survival mode, especially in times of pain, and keeps your focus on the future you want to create.

Benefits of Imagination

Imagination is a unique ability of the human mind. We do it so effortlessly that it sounds simple, but imagination is a

> Your state of mind, your brain, and the chemicals in your body are different depending on whether you see yourself in the reality of your best future or if you see yourself in your worst future. The mistake most people make is that they see what they want to avoid, not what they want to have.

complex function that activates a widespread area of the brain. When you see yourself in your best future with enough focus and emotion, you see it as your reality. Your state of mind, your brain, and the chemicals in your body are different depending on whether you see yourself in the reality of your best future or if you see yourself in your worst future.

The mistake most people make is that they see what they want to avoid, not what they want to have. But the more we try to avoid something, the more our mind comes back to it. This is how the mind works.

When you say "I want X" or "I don't want X," you see X in your mind in both cases. As Osho, the contemporary mystic, says, nature doesn't know negative terms. Nature only knows positive terms. For nature, a chair "is," a tree "is." The negative term "not" is an abstract idea that is a human creation. We can say "This is a chair," or "This is *not* a chair. This is a table." But nature only knows "This *is* a chair," and "This *is* a table." Nature does not know "This is *not* a chair." Naturally, when you say, "This is *not* a chair," your mind pictures a chair. So, you can't avoid the picture of a chair by adding the abstract idea of "not."

Psychology professor and founding father of thought suppression research, Dr. Daniel Wegner, did a simple and interesting experiment in the late 1980s. He was inspired by a quote from Fyodor Dostoevsky's *Winter Notes on Summer Impressions*: "Try to pose for yourself this task: not to think of a polar bear, and you will see that the cursed thing will come to mind every minute." Dr. Wegner decided to test this quote with an experiment.

You can do this experiment yourself. Try to not think of a polar bear for one or two minutes and see if you can avoid thinking about a polar bear. (Dr. Wegner's experiment stipulated not thinking of a polar bear for *five* minutes.)

Dr. Wegner's research shows that when we try to avoid a thought we can't do so, and it returns to our minds even more prominently later.[37]

So, it is best to use our powerful imaginal ability to picture our best future instead of focusing on avoiding an unwanted one.

When you see yourself in your best future and experience the happiness and joy it brings you, your body produces happy chemicals as if you are really living in that reality. Your brain cannot distinguish between what is happening in reality and what is happening in your imagination.

If you see yourself fulfilling your purpose—writing your book, making your music, opening your restaurant, starting your business, making your movie, starting your charity—your brain and your body behave as if it is already happening. It behaves as if you are already living in the desired reality. You see yourself differently. You perceive yourself differently. You will feel different.

Imagination opens you up to new possibilities.

Benefits of Drawing

When you draw your best future, you take this to another level. When you draw, the act of drawing activates both sides of your brain and engages a larger area of your brain.

When you draw, you make your dreams physical by committing them to paper. You emphasize them, making an impression on your brain. Thus you will remember them better. According to the "picture superiority effect," we remember pictures better than words. So when you draw, you remember what you've drawn better than when you talk or write about it. Drawing your best future makes your brain more focused on what you want to create. As you know, focus is the key.

With focus, you direct to your mind where to go and what to create.

Benefits of Singing

When you sing about your goals, you emphasize them in your mind even more.

When we sing, large areas of our brains are activated. Research shows that singing enhances the brain's neuroplasticity. In other words, singing helps our brains to work better.[38]

In fact, singing is one of the activities that may counteract the effects of aging on brain function in elderly individuals. There is also scientific research that shows the effectiveness of singing in treating neurological issues, such as stuttering, Parkinson's disease, autism, and acquired brain injury.[39] According to Professor Sarah Wilson from the School of Psychological Sciences at the University of Melbourne, "Singing is a form of natural therapy, it lifts our mood, releases dopamine and gives all those networks a workout, brining protective or neuro-protective benefits for our mental health."[40]

Singing has also been shown to release feel-good, healing chemicals, such as endorphins and oxytocin.[41] According to a research study conducted at the University of Frankfurt, singing also strengthens the immune system.[42]

In addition, singing connects us with ourselves on a deeper level. When you sing, you connect with your words in a more emotional way than when you speak them.

Attaching emotions to the words helps the words go deeper in your mind (the software) and wider in your brain (the hardware). It changes how the words are stored in your memory. I'm sure you've had the experience of hearing a song and immediately being reminded of a certain person or event.

Singing uses a larger area of your brain than simply speaking, making it a more effective way of sparking your creativity.

How to Do the *Design Your Best Future* Technique

To do this practice, get yourself a pleasing journal, and every morning after you get out of bed, before you start your activities for the day, take a few minutes to do the following steps.

Step 1: *Imagine your best future.*

Imagine your desired future. Imagine what you would like to do and how you would like to feel as your highest self in your best future. Imagine what you could accomplish if you focused on your best future rather than your current pain or discomfort.

To help you focus, ask yourself open-ended questions, such as the following:

"What is the best future that I want to have?"
"What is the thing that I really love to do?"
"How do I want to feel?"
"What would I like to do if I didn't have this pain or problem?"
"How would life feel if I would do what I really love to do?"
"What would my life be like if I was living based on my highest potential?"

Imagine your answers. See your best future clearly. See yourself living that desired future and feel how it feels. Imagine it vividly, as if you're already living that life, doing those things, feeling that way.

When you ask yourself an open-ended question, your brain starts searching its database of past experiences and knowledge to find the answer. Your brain actively looks to find an answer and it will strive to present you with new possibilities.

Visualize yourself in a positive state, a state that you wish to be in or achieve. If you have pain or discomfort in your body or mind, imagine yourself as completely healed. When we are going through difficulties, we know that it is not what we want. But we should also be clear about what we do want. Being clear about what you want gives your mind clear directions of where we want it to go. To accomplish any journey, you must first have a clear sense of your destination. It is necessary for growth as well.

Step 2: *Draw your best future.*

After you visualize your best future in your mind, draw a picture of yourself in that desired future. Draw simple figures of yourself in that desired life, feeling happy and fulfilled. Select two or three images that reflect that future and use stick figures (like the ones depicted in figure 9.1) or any other style you like, to illustrate an image of that future. Use crayons to add color and bring the drawing more to life.

Figure 9.1 Use stick figures to draw your best future.

Step 3: *Sing your best future.*

After visualizing and drawing your best future, sing about it. Sing how you feel about that future. You can improvise the words and melody each time or you can prepare the lyrics of what I call your *intention song* once and sing the same lyrics every time. Sing your intention song each morning and keep singing it throughout the day to elevate your mood.

After doing these 3 steps, think about what you can do today to move closer to that future. What step can you take? Imagine how much you would achieve in one year if you took one small step every day toward that future. And imagine how you would feel when you moved toward your best future with very little effort.

If getting closer to your future takes eating one healthy meal to support your health each day, do it. If it takes setting aside your phone and electronic devices for one moment and taking one *deep* breath, do it. If it takes writing one sentence for your book, do it. Do it and do it regularly because these actions add up.

It feels good when you do one small thing every day to take you closer to your goal. The reward center of your brain will be activated and because your brain always wants more reward, it will be motivated to continue moving toward your goal.

Feel the joy and satisfaction of your future self, visualize it, draw it, sing it, and take one small step toward it.

The *Design Your Best Future* Technique in Action

Jack is one of my meditation students. Recently he had a back surgery not long after his retirement from work. Having to stay home and rest to recover from the surgery, especially after more than forty years of work and being active, was boring to him, and the pain and inability to move much frustrated him. He had learned meditation from me less than a year before and was practicing his favorite technique every day to keep him in control of his mind and stay positive. However, he felt he could use more support to boost his mood.

He contacted me two weeks after his surgery to attend my G.R.O.W. program through phone calls to grow his motivation and sense of peace.

During the program he got clear about what he wanted to do next. He always had a dream of having a farm. But he was concerned whether with his condition after his surgery he would be able to perform the physical labor required for working the land. I thought the Design Your Best Future technique would be the perfect tool for him to keep his focus on his dream, to help him heal himself faster, and keep his motivation high to make his dream come true.

When I explained the technique, he liked it immediately. Just visualizing his farm, seeing himself building his farm, planting crops, looking after the horses and the chickens and the goats was enough to ignite the fire of his passion and bring him to a state of positivity required to see this vision fulfilled. By pumping the fuel of his passion even more with drawing and singing his best future, he created a sanctuary of positive feelings for himself. His focus became his farm and planning to make it happen.

He sang his intention song all day and that kept his focus on his best future and distracted him from his pain. His whole mind shifted. He wasn't bored or frustrated anymore. Now he had a purpose, a vision that was bigger than his temporary pain. He started planning every detail about his farm and how he wants to build it.

All this helped him through the journey of recovery with happiness and peace instead of boredom and frustration, and soon after he was back on his feet he started making his dream come true. He believes focusing on the future he wanted using this technique helped him immensely to stay positive and make his dream come true.

Jack's experience is a powerful example of how a simple shift in our mind and the right focus can change the flavor of our days and our results in life.

The Significance of the *Design Your Best Future* Technique

As we have discussed throughout, our minds are easily distracted and tend to focus on the negative. This is especially true when we are facing difficulties and challenges. We need effective tools to keep our focus on the positives, stay conscious of our purpose, and create the best future that we want and deserve. The strategy in this chapter is such a tool.

Life is a precious gift. Finding your purpose and the way of living that truly gives you joy and brings you fulfillment is an effective way to make the best use of this precious gift. Your future is not a fixed thing that happens to you. You create it and you alter it every moment by the decisions you make and the actions you take.

This technique helps you identify what you love to do and keeps your mind focused on it. It shifts your mind away from survival mode and into conscious mode.

Using your imagination to visualize, draw, and sing, engages wide areas of the brain and awakens your creativity. Creativity is an essential part of being human. It enhances your brain's capabilities and triggers the release of feel-good chemicals that are also healing. It relaxes your nervous system, lowers stress and anxiety, and boosts the immune system.

Moreover, when you activate your creativity you connect with your deeper self and open yourself to new possibilities.

Using the trinity of Imagine, Draw, Sing, you will have a happier mind and a healthier body. This trinity heals your pain in the moment while inspiring you to participate in creating the best future for yourself.

Life is a precious gift. Finding your purpose and the way of living that truly gives you joy and brings you fulfillment is an effective way to make the best use of this precious gift. Your future is not a fixed thing that happens to you. You create it and you alter it every moment by the decisions you make and the actions you take.

Life is a precious gift. And you deserve to enjoy this gift and to live your best life.

CONCLUSION: GROW UNTIL YOU BLOOM

LIFE IS GROWTH. Growth is life.

Growth is an essential part of life. At times, we may face problems or challenges, pains or difficulties, but if we move through our moments consciously, we will tap into our inner power to heal our pain and grow our lives in spite of them.

Problems and difficulties can be obstacles that stop us from living the life we want or, if we train our minds to see things with the right perspective, to see the bigger view, to see the positive disguised in the negative, they can become springboards to growth.

Even my biggest challenge, Lyme disease, did not hinder my growth. It fostered it. It taught me that each moment is a valuable gift and it is too precious to waste. And it inspired me to want to make the best use of the precious gift of my life.

I used the strategies and the wisdom shared in this book to keep my focus on the right mindset and see the bigger picture. I found these strategies and the wisdom behind them so effective and so grounding that I've taken them up as part of my daily routine and my lifestyle. And I've encouraged many others to do so.

Now, every day I get up and I ask, "What is my intention for today?" and "What is the best future that I want to create?" I use different strategies at different times during the day to keep my mind focused on creating the best future that I can imagine for myself and for others, while enjoying the gifts in the present moment.

My mission is to empower as many people as I can to live a happy, healthy, and purposeful life, to heal their pains and live their best life.

Because this is my purpose, I teach meditation classes and offer private coaching sessions for my students and my clients. I conduct workshops and programs for communities, organizations, and companies to share science-based wisdom and techniques to grow their happiness and their success, to reduce stress, and improve productivity. I write articles for magazines and share tips and inspirational suggestions for reducing stress and improving well-being. I've just finished writing my first book, but it will not be my last book. I will keep writing and sharing the treasures that I have gathered from the greatest masters on the planet throughout the years.

As mentioned previously, I also created a program called G.R.O.W., an acronym for Get clarity, Respond, Optimize, and Wisdom, to coach and guide you to grow your mind and grow your life. It is a 4-step process that gives you happiness, peace, and positivity in your mind and clarity, focus, and greater success in your life.

I am still creating more models, techniques, and programs that I will continue to share.

The challenges in my life were definitely not a hindrance but rather a springboard to my growth. Everything I've accomplished after my illness is because Lyme disease was my wake-up call. It was a blessing in disguise.

If you are facing a problem or challenge, or you are feeling overwhelmed by the speed of modern life, you may have a blessing in disguise, too. It may not be immediately clear to you, but once you see the bigger picture, you will notice that what you have perceived as an obstacle is really contributing to your growth.

> I believe there is a creative power inside you and it should be used. A flower reaches its full potential when it blooms. You have the capacity to bloom and you will feel good when you fulfill your potential. If you are not feeling fulfilled, you have more potential inside you waiting to be fulfilled.

When you see and focus on the bigger purpose in your life, you will be more inspired to grow yourself to your highest potential and live your best life.

Our time on this planet, no matter how long it is, is still short. It is to be enjoyed and used to create the best life that you can imagine. I believe there is a creative power inside you and it should be used.

A flower reaches its full potential when it blooms. You have the capacity to bloom and you will feel good when you fulfill your potential. If you are not feeling fulfilled, you have more potential

> Every day when you wake up, ask yourself, "How can I be happy today? How can I be today to be happy? What can I do today to bring a smile to someone else's face? What can I do today to take a step toward my best future?"

inside you waiting to be fulfilled. To me, this is a good sign. It shows that you have more and *are* more than you think. You need to keep growing until you bloom to your fullest potential.

In nature, plants grow as much as their environment allows. They don't hold back. If a plant doesn't hold back, why should you?

If you live your life in conscious mode rather than survival mode, you won't hold back. You will grow and progress. You will strive to expand yourself and step into the unknown. As the branch of a tree grows when it stretches itself into spaces it has never been before, so will you grow by stretching out from your comfort zone.

The branch of a tree is growing every day even though we don't notice it. It grows, but it grows in a relaxed way. It grows persistently, but without stress. As Lao Tzu teaches, "Nature does not hurry, yet everything is accomplished."

With simple and effective strategies, we can learn from nature and keep growing and blooming by stretching out from our comfort zone while remaining relaxed.

Every day when you wake up, ask yourself, "How can I be happy today? How can I *be* today to be happy? What can I do today to bring a smile to someone else's face? What can I do today to take a step toward my best future?" By asking yourself these questions, you will live a happy and purposeful life.

Your mind will guide you if you ask it to. You just need to commit to asking and then do what your mind and your heart say.

The strategies in this book will support you, shifting your mind to the creative zone, the growth zone, the healing zone, the conscious zone. Everything I have shared with you in this book will help you to create a happy mind and a happy life, to grow your mind and grow your life.

Now is the beginning of the rest of your journey. I wish you growth, happiness, and fulfillment. And remember: Grow your mind to grow your life; create a happy mind to create a happy life.

MY GIFTS TO YOU

ARE YOU READY to create your best life one drop of focus at a time?

Visit www.drnarjes.com/gift to access an action plan and series of worksheets designed to show you step-by-step how to implement the seven strategies and create a focused mind that empowers you to unlock your best life. Use these materials to support you on your journey to a happy mind and a happy life.

On my website, www.drnarjes.com, you will find more resources to help you heal your pain and create your best life:

- Published magazine articles and other writings
- Online courses
- Guided meditations
- Meditation courses
- Coaching programs
- And more . . .

ACKNOWLEDGMENTS

I AM GRATEFUL that this book has given me the chance to share my passion in life with you.

There were many people without whom none of this would be possible, and I want to express my gratitude to them.

First, I would like to thank all my teachers who gave me the precious gift of wisdom and helped me grow. I send my deepest gratitude to my teacher, Vikas Malkani, who introduced me to the path of wisdom and who was instrumental in shaping me into who I am today. Vikas, I will be forever grateful to you. And thank you for kindly agreeing to write the foreword.

I would also like to thank everyone who has supported me on this journey of life through my highs and lows.

The first among them is Farshid, my loving and beloved husband and partner in life. Thank you, Farshid, for being my rock and support on this beautiful journey. Many people who know us think that we love Japan so much because we first met in Japan, and we know that there is some truth in that.

I want to express my gratitude to Patricia King, a California-based writer-editor, for the time she spent reading the first draft of this book and giving her valuable and generous comments.

I wish to thank my editor, Julia Pastore, for the pleasure of working with her on this project. Julia gave careful, honest, and sharp comments and asked the right questions to help the message come across clearly.

I also want to thank my copy editor, Juliann Barbato, for her kind support of my work.

And I would like to express my deepest gratitude to my parents, whose unconditional love and support nurtured my wish to grow to my highest potential. They believed in me, encouraged me to follow my dreams, and provided all the resources and opportunities possible to support me in doing so. Words cannot express my gratitude for my parents.

Special thanks to all the wonderful people who supported this work with their generous endorsements.

And finally, I'd like to thank my students and clients who gave me the honor of serving them to fulfill my life purpose. I grew by helping them grow. And special thanks to those who shared their personal experiences with my techniques and strategies and gave me permission to include them in this book.

And I would like to thank you for reading what I shared in this book and letting me make a contribution to your growth!

ENDNOTES

Chapter 2: From Survival Mode to Conscious Mode

1   Bruce H. Lipton, *The Biology of Belief: Unleashing the Power of Consciousness, Matter & Miracles* (Sydney: Hay House Australia, 2016).

2   Jon Kabat-Zinn, *Full Catastrophe Living: Using the Wisdom of Your Body and Mind to Face Stress, Pain, and Illness* (New York: Bantam Books, 2013).

3   F. Zeidan, S. K. Johnson, et al., "Mindfulness Meditation Improves Cognition: Evidence of Brief Mental Training," *Consciousness and Cognition* 19, no. 2 (June 2010): 597–605.

4   I. Lebuda, D. L. Zabelina, et al., "Mind Full of Ideas: A Meta-analysis of the Mindfulness-Creativity Link," *Personality and Individual Differences* 93 (April 2016): 22–26.

5   D. S. Black, G. A. O'Reilly, et al., "Mindfulness Meditation and Improvement in Sleep Quality and Daytime Impairment among Older Adults with Sleep Disturbances," *JAMA Internal Medicine* 175, no. 4 (April 1, 2015): 494–501.

6   Jon Kabat-Zinn, Lesley Lipworth, et al. (1985). "The Clinical Use of Mindfulness Meditation for the Self-Regulation of Chronic Pain," *Journal of Behavioral Medicine* 8, no. 2 (June 1985):163–90.

7   D. S. Black and G. M. Slavich, "Mindfulness Meditation and the Immune System: A Systematic Review of Randomized Controlled Trials," *Annals of the New York Academy of Science* 1373, no. 1 (June 2016): 113–24.

8   S. Lazar et al., "Meditation Experience Is Associated with Increased Cortical Thickness," *Neuroreport* 16, no. 17 (November 28, 2005): 1893–97.

9   B. K. Hölzel, J. Carmody, et al., "Mindfulness Practice Leads to Increases in Regional Brain Gray Matter Density," *Psychiatry Research: Neuroimaging* 191, no. 1 (January 30, 2011): 36–43.

10   B. K. Hölzel et al., "Stress Reduction Correlates with Structural Changes in the Amygdala," *Social Cognitive and Affective Neuroscience* 5, no. 1 (March 2010): 11–17.

11   Swami Rama, *Happiness Is Your Creation* (Honesdale, PA: Himalayan Institute Press, 2005).

Chapter 3: Refine Your Limiting Beliefs

12   Marianne Szegedy-Maszak, "Mysteries of the Mind: Your Unconscious Is Making Your Everyday Decisions," *U.S. News & World Report*, February 28, 2005.

13   M. Zimmerman, "Neurophysiology of Sensory Systems," in *Fundamentals of Sensory Physiology*, ed. Robert F. Schmidt (Berlin: Springer-Verlag, 1986).

14   J. D. Levine, N. C. Gordon, et al., "The Mechanism of Placebo Analgesia," *The Lancet*, 312, no. 8091 (September 23,1978):654–57.

15   J. B. Moseley, K. O'Malley, et al., "A Controlled Trial of Arthroscopic Surgery for Osteoarthritis of the Knee," *New England Journal of Medicine*, 347, no. 2 (July 11, 2002):81–88.

16   Anita Moorjani, *Dying to Be Me: My Journey from Cancer, to Near Death, to True Healing* (Sydney: Hay House Australia, 2018).

Chapter 4: Create Mindful Distraction

17   *Mindful Distraction* is a proprietary concept and technique created by Dr. Narjes Gorjizadeh.

18   Deloitte, *2017 Global Mobile Consumer Survey: US Edition* (July 2017): 3, www.deloitte.com/us/mobileconsumer.

19   A. K. Przybylski and N. Weinstein, "Can You Connect with Me Now? How the Presence of Mobile Communication Technology Influences Face-to-Face Conversation Quality," *Journal of Personal and Social Relationships* 30, no. 3 (July 19, 2012): 237–46.

20   M. A. Killingsworth and D. T. Gilbert, "A Wandering Mind Is an Unhappy Mind," *Science* 330 no. 6006 (November 12, 2010): 932.

Chapter 5: Embrace Gratitude

21   R. A. Emmons and M. E. McCullough, "Counting Blessings versus Burdens: An Experimental Investigation of Gratitude and Subjective Well-Being in Daily Life," *Journal of Personality and Social Psychology* 84, no.2 (February 2003): 377–89.

22   J. A. Rash, M. K. Matsuba, et al., "Gratitude and Well-Being: Who Benefits the Most from a Gratitude Intervention?," *Applied Psychology: Health and Well-Being* 3, no. 3 (November 2011): 350–69.

23   S. C. Segerstrom, S. E. Taylor, et al., "Optimism Is Associated with Mood, Coping, and Immune Change in Response to Stress," *Journal of Personality and Social Psychology* 74, no. 6 (1998): 1646–55.

24   A. M. Wood, S. Joseph, et al., "Gratitude Influences Sleep through the Mechanism of Pre-sleep Cognitions," *Journal of Psychosomatic Research* 66, no. 1 (January 2009): 43–48.

25   M. E. McCullough, R. A. Emmons, et al., "The Grateful Disposition: A Conceptual and Empirical Topography," *Journal of Personality and Social Psychology,* 82, no. 1 (January 1, 2002): 112–27.

26   R. A. Emmons and M. E. McCullough, "Counting Blessings versus Burdens: An Experimental Investigation of Gratitude and Subjective Well-Being in Daily Life," *Journal of Personality and Social Psychology* 84, no. 2 (February 2003): 377–89.

27   R. A. Emmons, "Gratitude, Subjective Well-Being, and the Brain," in *The Science of Subjective Well-Being*, eds. M. Eid and R. Larsen (New York: Guilford Press, 2008).

28   Eckhart Tolle, *The Power of Now: A Guide to Spiritual Enlightenment* (Sydney: Hachette Australia, 2011).

Chapter 6: Describe the Moment

29   *Describe the Moment* is a proprietary technique created by Dr. Narjes Gorjizadeh.

Chapter 7: Make Conscious Choices

30   Bronnie Ware, *The Top Five Regrets of the Dying: A Life Transformed by the Dearly Departing* (Carlsbad, CA: Hay House, 2012).

Chapter 8: Emphasize the Positive

31   *Emphasize the Positive* is a proprietary technique created by Dr. Narjes Gorjizadeh.

32   L. M. Williams, J. M. Gatt, et al., "'Negativity Bias' in Risk for Depression and Anxiety: Brain-Body Fear Circuitry Correlates, 5-HTT-LPR and Early Life Stress," *Neuroimage* 47, no. 3 (September 2009): 804–14.

33   D. Kahneman and A. Tversky, "Prospect Theory: An Analysis of Decision under Risk," *Econometrica* 47, no. 2 (March 1979): 263–92.

34   R. F. Baumeister, E. Bratslavsky, et al., "Bad Is Stronger Than Good," *Review of General Psychology* 5, no. 4 (December 1, 2001): 323–70.

Chapter 9: Design Your Best Future

35   Patti Dobrowolski, "Draw Your Future," TEDx Talks, January 10, 2012, www.youtube.com/watch?v=zESeeaFDVSw.

36   *Design Your Best Future* is a proprietary technique created by Dr. Narjes Gorjizadeh.

37   D. M. Wegner, D. J. Schneider, et al., "Paradoxical Effects of Thought Suppression," *Journal of Personality and Social Psychology* 53, no. 1 (1987): 5–13.

38   C. Y. Wan and G. Schlaug, G., "Music Making as a Tool for Promoting Brain Plasticity across the Life Span," *Neuroscientist* 16, no. 5 (October 2010): 566–77.

39   C. Y. Wan, T. Rüber, et al., "The Therapeutic Effects of Singing in Neurological Disorders," *Music Perception* 27, no. 4 (April 2010): 287–95.

40   www.abc.net.au/classic/read-and-watch/how-music-works/how-music-works-what-happens-to-your-brain-when-you-sing/10115596.

41   J. Kang, A. Scholp, et al., "A Review of the Physiological Effects and Mechanisms of Singing," *Journal of Voice* 32, no. 4 (July 2018): 390–95.

42   G. Kreutz, S. Bongard, et al., "Effects of Choir Singing or Listening on Secretory Immunoglobulin A, Cortisol, and Emotional state," *Journal of Behavioral Medicine* 27, no. 6 (December 2004): 623–35.

ABOUT THE AUTHOR

DR. NARJES GORJIZADEH is a PhD research scientist, certified meditation and mindfulness teacher, life coach, and global speaker.

She received her PhD degree in materials science from Tōhoku University in Japan. As a research scientist, she spent nearly two decades exploring the science of materials.

At a crossroads in her personal and professional life, she encountered meditation and the science of the mind and has spent the past ten years studying both to create a unique model for achieving a happy and stress-free life. Bridging the gap between ancient wisdom and modern science, her innovative strategies and unique teaching style promote peace and positivity in mind, and clarity, focus, and greater success in life. Dr. Narjes is the creator of the G.R.O.W. program and several breakthrough concepts such as *Mindful Distraction*, *Describe the Moment*, and *Design Your Best Future*. Her work has touched thousands of lives around the world. In her programs, workshops, online courses, and private coaching, she helps individuals and employees of companies train their mind to increase their focus, inner peace, and productivity to unlock their highest potential and live their best life.

Dr. Narjes has been featured in several international magazines on wellness and personal growth, including *LifePositive*, India's number 1 magazine for personal and spiritual growth, and *LivingNow*, Australia's largest holistic magazine.

Her mission is to empower every person with science-based wisdom and practical tools to create a life of happiness, success, and fulfillment.

For more on Dr. Narjes, visit www.drnarjes.com. For inquiries about training, coaching, or speaking, contact her at narjes@drnarjes.com.

LinkedIn:
www.linkedin.com/in/dr-narjes

Facebook:
www.facebook.com/narjes.gorjizadeh1

Printed in Great Britain
by Amazon